other books by Ronald J. Sider:

Andreas Bodenstein von Karlstadt: The Development of His Thought (1517-1525). "Studies in Medieval and Reformation Thought," No. 11. Leiden: Brill, 1974.

The Chicago Declaration. Carol Stream, Ill.: Creation House, 1974.

Christ and Violence. Scottdale, Pa.: Herald Press, 1979.

The Graduated Tithe. Downers Grove, Ill.: InterVarsity Press, 1978.

Karlstadt's Battle with Luther. Philadelphia: Fortress Press, 1978.

Rich Christians in an Age of Hunger: A Biblical Study. Downers Grove, Ill.: InterVarsity Press, 1977.

LIVING MORE SIMPLY

BIBLICAL PRINCIPLES & PRACTICAL MODELS

EDITED BY
RONALD J. SIDER

INTER-VARSITY PRESS
DOWNERS GROVE
ILLINOIS 60515

796

InterVarsity Press is the book-publishing division of
Inter-Varsity Christian Fellowship,
a student movement active on campus at
hundreds of universities, colleges and schools of
nursing. For information about local and
regional activities, write IVCF,
233 Langdon St., Madison, WI 53703.

Distributed in Canada through InterVarsity Press,
1875 Leslie St., Unit 10, Don Mills, Ontario M3B 2M5, Canada.

All Scripture quotations, unless otherwise indicated,
are from the Revised Standard Version of the
Bible, copyrighted 1946, 1952, © 1971, 1973.

All Scripture quotations marked NIV are from the New
International Version of the Bible. Copyright © 1978 by
the New York International Bible Society.
Used by permission of Zondervan Bible Publishers.

All Scripture quotations marked KJV are from the
King James Version of the Bible.

"Spare and Share" is a pamphlet produced by the Mennonite
Central Committee and reprinted here by permission.

For the poem by James Weldon Johnson on pp. 110-11:
Copyright: Edward B. Marks Music Corporation. Used by Permission.

ISBN 0-87784-808-4
Library of Congress Catalog Card Number: 79-3634

Printed in the United States of America

ACKNOWLEDGMENTS

Special thanks go to John R. W. Stott for proposing the idea of a Consultation on Simple Lifestyle and to Horace Fenton, Jr., who graciously gave time as co-coordinator of both the U.S. and International Consultations.

Gerald Anderson, director of the Overseas Ministries Study Center, kindly offered his center's excellent facilities (plus generous financial assistance) for the U.S. Consultation on Simple Lifestyle.

I want also to thank the planning committee for the U.S. Consultation on Simple Lifestyle:

John F. Alexander	Mark Hatfield	Richard Mouw
Malcolm Barnum	Michael Haynes	Mary Pioche
Wayne Bragg	Randolph Jones	Wyn Potter
Allan C. Emery	Jay Kessler	Russ Reid
		Jayne Millar Wood

Special thanks go to Marilyn Carlstrom, administrative assistant to Wayne Bragg at Wheaton College's program on Human Needs and Global Resources. She provided excellent editorial assistance at very short notice.

This consultation and book would not have been possible without Mark Cerbone, my assistant in both the U.S. and International Consultations. Donating his time as a Mennonite Central Committee Voluntary Service person, Mark has given superb administrative, organizational and secretarial assistance. I am profoundly grateful for the gift of two years of his life to the cause of developing greater evangelical concern for simple lifestyles.

All income from royalties from this book will go to the ongoing activity of the Unit on Ethics and Society of the Theological Commission of the World Evangelical Fellowship.

PARTICIPANTS AT THE U.S. CONSULTATION
ON SIMPLE LIFESTYLE

John F. Alexander
Anne Allen
Elaine Amerson
Gerald H. Anderson
Ramez Atallah
Michael Ballard
Malcolm M. Barnum
David J. Bosch
Ann Bragg
Wayne Bragg
Mark Cerbone
Karen Coote
Ann Dahl
Howard A. Dahl
Peter H. Davids
Charles Day
Dora DeMoss
Robert DeMoss
Richard Dugger
Mrs. Richard Dugger
Allan C. Emery, Jr.
Mrs. Allan Emery, Jr.
Samuel Escobar
Norman Ewert
Margaret R. Feaver
Helen Fenton
Horace Fenton, Jr.
Louis C. Fischer
Frank Gaebelein
Art Gish
Vic Glavach
Jørgen Glenthøj
Michael Haynes

Faith Hershberger
John Hoehn
Marion Hoehn
Esther D. Horner
Norman A. Horner
Richard Jacobson
Shirley Jacobson
Frances Jackson
Diane R. Jepsen
Benny Joseph
J. Andrew Kirk
Carolyn Klaus
Ronald L. Klaus
Geoffrey Kotzen
Charette B. Kvernstoen
John Kyle
Lois Kyle
Doris Longacre
Charles Massey
Claity Massey
Don McClanen
Ron McDonald
Jane Medema
Ken Medema
Elizabeth Miller
Harry Mills
George Monsma, Jr.
Charles Neder
Susan Neder
Bruce Nicholls
Beatrice Nichols
Bruce Nichols
Lois Ottaway

René Padilla
James Parker
William Pennell
Beaver Perkins
Elizabeth Poppinga
David T. Pullen
Nancy Jo Pullen
Todd E. Putney
Grace Roberts
W. Dayton Roberts
Joe Roos
Ann Rowe
Vinay Samuel
Robert R. Schuyler
Waldron Scott
Lois Shaw
Mark R. Shaw
Arbutus B. Sider
Ronald J. Sider
Karen Simon
Pinkie Sitoy
T. Valentino Sitoy, Jr.
Sarah E. Small
Virginia Strigas
Elaine Tanis
Maribeth Vander Weele
Joan Vogt
Virgil Vogt
Carol Westphal
Dennis Wood
Jayne Millar Wood

INTRODUCTION

Ronald J. Sider

When Billy Graham and Hudson Armerding called together about eighty evangelical leaders in Atlanta in December 1977 for a Consultation on Future Evangelical Concerns, the question of a simpler lifestyle frequently surfaced. The reaction was always positive. We agreed that the urgent need for increased efforts in evangelism and development call for sacrificial giving. Global economic trends also require reduced consumption by the affluent. Then, about the fourth time the issue of a simpler lifestyle emerged, Loren Cunningham, president of Youth With A Mission, made a crucial comment: "Yes, I believe the evangelical community is ready to adopt a simpler lifestyle—*if* we evangelical leaders will model it." That ended the discussion of simpler lifestyle.

Millions of Christians also have come to see the need for simpler lifestyles. What they want now are concrete, practical suggestions and specific, workable models. "Don't give us more theory and good advice. Don't lay another guilt trip on us. Give us good personal examples and concrete models that we can consider, pray about and adapt to our unique setting." Exciting, concrete models are emerging.

Consider Eastminster Presbyterian Church in Wichita, Kansas. At the beginning of 1976, that suburban church had an ambitious and expensive church construction program in the works. Their architect had prepared a $525,000 church building design. Then a devastating earthquake struck in Guatemala on February 4, destroying thousands of homes and buildings. Many evangelical congregations lost their churches.

When Eastminster's board of elders met shortly after the Guatemalan tragedy, a layperson posed a simple question: "How can we set out to buy an ecclesiastical Cadillac when our brothers and sisters in Guatemala have just lost their little Volkswagen?"

The board of elders courageously opted for a dramatic change of plans. They slashed their building program by about two-thirds and settled for $180,000 worth of church construction. The church sent their pastor and two elders to Guatemala to see how they could help. When they returned and reported tremendous need, the church borrowed $120,000 from a local bank and rebuilt twenty-six Guatemalan churches and twenty-eight Guatemalan pastors' houses.

The last few years have been years of tremendous growth for Eastminster—in spiritual vitality, concern for missions and, yes, in attendance and budget as well. I talked recently with Dr. Frank Kik, Eastminster's pastor. Eastminster is staying in close touch with church developments in Central America and has recently pledged $40,000 to an evangelical seminary there. Cutting their building program to share with needy sisters and brothers in Guatemala "meant far more to Eastminster Presbyterian than to Guatemala," Dr. Kik said.

That Kansas church is only one example. There are many other examples of churches living more simply. Diverse, practical models for individuals, families and professional persons are also becoming more numerous. The collection and publication of some of those models was a major goal of the U.S. Consultation on Simple Lifestyle held at Ventnor, New Jersey, in April 1979.

The story of the U.S. Consultation on Simple Lifestyle began in 1974 at the Lausanne Congress for World Evangelization. The Lausanne Congress, probably the largest, most representative, international gathering of evangelical Christians ever assembled, summoned Christians to renewed commitment to the evangelistic task. The Lausanne Covenant, drawn up at the congress and subsequently signed by thousands of Christians in all parts of the world, outlined the things deemed necessary for effective worldwide evangelism in the late twentieth century. One of them was that affluent Christians begin to live simpler lifestyles. Paragraph 9 of the Lausanne Covenant reads:

All of us are shocked by the poverty of millions and disturbed by the injustices which cause it. Those of us who live in affluent circumstances accept our duty to develop a simple lifestyle in order to contribute generously to both relief and evangelism.[1]

The Lausanne Covenant states the proper motivation for simpler living. Christians are not committed to a simple lifestyle. We are committed to Jesus Christ and his kingdom and thus to faithful participation in the mission of our servant King in a lost, broken world. It is because more than two and a half billion people have never heard the gospel and because up to one billion are starving or malnourished that Western Christians today must drastically simplify our lifestyles.

Over sixty percent of those two and a half billion persons who have not heard of Jesus Christ live in social groupings and sub-nations where the church has not yet effectively taken root. Cross-cultural missionaries are needed. Gottfried Osei-Mensah, executive secretary of the Lausanne Committee on World Evangelization, recently proposed that every one thousand evangelicals should send one missionary couple to such unreached peoples. If that is to be done, affluent Christians must adopt simpler lifestyles.

The reality of world hunger also raises questions about affluent lifestyles. The World Food Council recently reported that "up to one-third of all children born alive die from malnutrition or [malnutrition-induced] diseases before the age of five." In 1977 the National Academy of Sciences published a study stating that "seven hundred and fifty million people in the poorest nations live in extreme poverty with annual incomes of less than $75." In the U.S., on the other hand, middle-class people often feel poor when they make only $15,000, $18,000 or even $25,000 each year.[2] We are fourteen times as rich as the average person in India, and the gap continues to widen.

Asceticism is not a biblical ideal. This created world is a magnificently beautiful gift from our Father and he intends us to enjoy and care for it. As the Lausanne Covenant reminds us, however, biblical people should do that in a way that does not neglect the obligations to proclaim the gospel, care for the needy and seek justice for the oppressed. In a world dramatically divided between rich and poor, the pledge of the Lausanne Covenant is desperately urgent: "Those of us who live in affluent circumstances accept our duty to develop a simple lifestyle in order to contribute generously to both relief and evangelism."

As John R. W. Stott (one of the key framers of the Lausanne Covenant) traveled throughout the world after that 1974 congress, he was asked by Third-World Christians if Western

Christians really meant the statement on simple lifestyle in the Lausanne Covenant. So John Stott proposed an International Consultation on Simple Lifestyle. Subsequent discussion between Stott's Lausanne Theology and Education Group and the Unit on Ethics and Society (of which I serve as convenor) of the Theological Commission of the World Evangelical Fellowship led to a decision to have these two groups cosponsor an International Consultation on Simple Lifestyle in London in March 1980.[3]

Preparations for the International Consultation on Simple Lifestyle include scores of local study groups around the world. It was also decided to hold a preparatory U.S. Consultation in 1979.

In April 25-29, 1979, about one hundred evangelicals met in Ventnor, New Jersey, at the Overseas Ministries Study Center (which generously supported the Consultation) to explore the implications of the Lausanne Covenant's call for a simple lifestyle. During those five days, which seemed unusually blessed with the presence of the Holy Spirit, the papers and models printed in this book were presented. After a moving keynote address by William Pannell (chapter one), papers by Frank Gaebelein (chapter two) and Peter Davids (chapter three) focused on the biblical foundations. Gladys Hunt (chapter seven) and George Monsma (chapter eight) showed how the urgent needs both for economic justice and worldwide evangelistic outreach summon affluent Christians to live more simply. Each morning we were challenged by specific models of simple lifestyle: in the family (chapter four), in the church (chapter five) and in professional life (chapter six). Throughout the entire consultation, pianist/soloist Ken Medema sang the message of the consultation into our hearts and souls with his stirring songs and marvelous improvisations.

The papers printed here reflect the desire of the one hundred people who gathered for the U.S. Consultation on

Simple Lifestyle to share with others their developing visions and groping attempts at implementation. The most basic question raised by the Consultation and the papers is a simple one: will we dare to measure our lifestyles by the needs of the poor and unevangelized rather than by the living standards of our affluent neighbors?

Notes

[1]Copies of the Lausanne Covenant, accompanied by an exposition by John R. W. Stott, can be purchased by writing to the Lausanne Committee for World Evangelization, P.O. Box 1100, Wheaton, IL 60187, U.S.A.

[2]S. Fraker, et al., "The Middle-Class Poor," *Newsweek*, 12 Sept. 1977, pp. 30-31.

[3]*Co-coordinators:* Ronald J. Sider and Horace Fenton, Jr. *Planning Committee Members:* Ramez Atallah, Saphir Athyal, Sir Frederick Catherwood, P. T. Chandapilla, Harvie Conn, Leighton Ford, Donald E. Hoke, Festo Kivengere, Samuel Moffett, George Monsma, Jr., René Padilla, Russ Reid, John R. W. Stott.

A CALL
TO A
SIMPLER
LIFESTYLE

William E. Pannell

1

I have been tremendously impressed by the recent revolution in Iran.* It is important not because it provides our leaders with an explanation for our discomfort at the gas pumps. It is important not because it is a new phenomenon nor because it is tidy and without sin. It is none of those. It may not even succeed, especially in ways congenial to North Americans.

THE DREAM
The revolution is important because it is a dramatic attempt of a people to create a context, a system in which it is possible to celebrate on their own terms and by their own definitions a sense of who they are—a sense of "somebodiness" as we would call it in the black community.

The revolution is instructive because it reflects an ancient

---

*Author's note: This material was written in the spring of 1979 and is not intended to condone the terrorism of more recent times (December, 1979).

dream shared both by the human race and by God himself. The dream is for a society in which it is possible for men and women to celebrate the meaning of their humanity in the secure embrace of love and justice. The West is made uncomfortable because this attempt is made by rejecting Western definitions of the good life and the implicit assumptions of racial and cultural superiority that underlie it. We are confused because our State Department and CIA, to say nothing of oil company moguls, have seriously underestimated the power of religions to effect change in a secular world. There is a connection between that ongoing drama and simpler lifestyle, for it provides one opportunity to view, indeed to feel, the heartache of our world society. That heartache is the larger, organizing context for our discussions.

The question of lifestyle might not have come so close, or presented itself so forcibly to me, had I not moved to Southern California. As you know, Southern California *is* lifestyle. It is the mystique and tragedy of San Clemente with its hermitlike ex-President and nearby, the eerie conelike shapes with their promise of a nuclear solution to the state's energy needs. Southern California, at the other end of a long corridor, is also Palm Springs with its plush golf courses sprawled at the foot of craggy mountains; it is the good life luxuriously nestled along Bob Hope Drive. One can slip easily into a condominium there beginning around $110,000, with, of course, maid service provided.

Somewhere between San Clemente and Palm Springs there is something for everyone, and style is the thing. Hear it in the names: Malibu, Newport Beach, Bel Air, Beverly Hills; or Watts, East Los Angeles and Pasadena—the city that once a year plucks petals off living things and creatively pastes them on the sides of monstrous floats depicting life as they think it ought to be.

I feel a bit awkward discussing this topic because I do not have the question of lifestyle sufficiently answered in my own mind and experience. I wrestle with it, not primarily because of my location (Pasadena), but because I too have been crowded by events, pushed by history, to consider the unthinkable. And I must say that I do not always like what I'm forced to consider. That is due in part to the fact that the people from my side of town and with my background always thought they invented simple lifestyle. What some people are now calling for, in the name of alternatives, we were born to: heat from wood or coal, or solar heat upstairs (when there was any upstairs at all), a huge garden behind the house and transportation by one's own locomotion.

It is something of a quirk in history that at a time when some of you are calling for a simple life, for whatever reasons, some of us are just beginning to taste a bit of the good life. I suspect that dimension of the issue causes considerable pain among our brothers and sisters abroad. At the point in their history when they are beginning to emerge from colonial bondage into the "first, fine, careless rapture" of self-determination, they are hearing their former tormentors urging cutbacks and pointing to a need for reduction in human expectations. It's enough to make nonwhite people downright suspicious. Why are persons of color now being asked to rein in their hopes? Because white people are a bit inconvenienced. Of course the issue is more profound than that, though I am not willing to let go of that notion. It provides a necessary perspective.

THE TEXT

It is my understanding that our text, though perhaps not enjoying the status of inerrancy, is from the Lausanne Covenant. Let me remind you of that portion germane to our gathering: "All of us are shocked by the poverty of millions and disturbed by the injustices which cause it. Those of us who live in affluent circumstances accept our duty to develop a simple lifestyle in order to contribute generously to both relief and evangelism."

That is, it seems to me, a remarkably restrained statement. Further, it seems overly optimistic in its confident assertion that affluent people accept their duty to develop a simple lifestyle. That may be true of some people but not all. The statement is also noteworthy in its attempt to make a connection between lifestyle and evangelism and relief.

Yet the Lausanne statement seems incredibly bland in the face of our human situation. What seems clearly at issue today, at least for most of humanity, is neither relief nor evangelism, but survival itself. The future of the human race is at stake. My saying that is not an attempt to become an evangelical Heilbroner.[1] Outside the province of those in control ("the unyoung, uncolored, unpoor"), most of the world already knows that. Their plight is well known. No one of us who lives in affluence can ignore the despicable circumstances of black people in South Africa or the horrible torture of citizens of Paraguay, Uruguay and Brazil or the suffering of the poor at the hands of their rapacious benefactors in the Dominican Republic and Nicaragua. For such people —and millions more like them—survival is the only word which even comes close to their aspirations.

We know something about the scenario. We have read Ronald Sider and Arthur Simon.[2] When that got a bit stiff, we turned to Stan Mooneyham of World Vision—and ran into the same grim realities. Humanity is hurting and nature is fed up. That combination of words sets some of our agenda or at least shapes the context.

I was impressed by a speech given by Rosemary Radford Reuther at Brown University's baccalaureate last June. In it she stressed the connection between the welfare of humankind and the health of the ecosystem. She said:

In the biblical view, the raping of nature and the exploitation of people in society are profoundly understood as part of one reality, creating disaster in both. We look not to the past but to a new future, brought about by social repentance and conversion to divine commandments, so that the covenant of creation can be rectified and God's Shalom brought to nature and society. Just as the fact of nature and society grows hostile through injustice, so it will be restored to harmony through righteousness. The biblical understanding of nature, therefore, inheres in a human ethical vision, a vision of ecojustice, in which the enmity or harmony of nature with humanity is part of the human historical drama of good and evil.[3]

THE CONTEXT

Reuther advances her view of the Judeo-Christian perspective against (1) the romantic neo-animism suggested by Theodore Roszak (Where the Wasteland Ends) and (2) certain equally romantic conservatives seeking to resolve the ecological crisis by redefining theology so as to extend the mandate of human dominion to include stewardship. In her perception of such attempts to deal with a new agenda forced on us by the natural environment, Reuther observes that neither option takes seriously the economic system which exploits "classes, races and nations" in its use of natural resources. Exploitation of people and resources must be seen as part and parcel of the problem. She contends, I think rightly, that "both the romantic and the conservationist approaches never deal with the question of ecojustice; namely, the reordering of access to and use of natural resources within a just economy." I like her observation that "it is no accident that nature is most devastated where poor people live."

John Neuhaus, the erstwhile activist/theologian/editor, cautions us against an uncritical acceptance of the doomsayers' vision. He reminds us that, while the human and ecological situation is grim, there are signs that it may not be so hopeless as the prophets say it is. Besides, he asserts, there is historical precedent that in time of crisis unforeseen events can occur which avert impending disasters. "If in 1870 you could have fed available information into a computer you could have confidently predicted that by 1900 the city of New York would be lost under 100 feet of horse manure. In 1870 that would have seemed a fair scientific assumption."[4] It didn't happen, of course, and Neuhaus and others assert that the reason it didn't is because in the intervening years certain critical, unforeseen changes occurred which altered the course of history. The argument is effective: if it happened once—and of course it has happened more than once —then dramatic changes altering even our gloomiest prophecies can occur again. Indeed they should be expected.

The argument that things are not so bad as the doomsayers think, or more important, that remedies are already at hand, raises the more fundamental question: "If indeed we have the scientific and technological genius to rectify the situation, why don't we?" The two issues, ecology and ethics, go hand in hand. Barbara Ward put it well in *Justice in a Human Environment*:

> *Mankind's environmental reality–and ecology as a part of that reality–are in no way separate from the problems of justice and development. Part of the significance of the whole environmental issue for Christians is that it does help us once again to see our planet in all its interdependence, to see it as the arena of human destiny, and to take our environmental background as part of our broader perception of justice.*[5]

Ward is especially helpful in her treatment of the environmental question in context. That context is composed of "man's ethical, social and moral environment and ... the natural environment of our physical cosmos."

In a fine appraisal, Ward says:

*The remarkable fact about the present period of history
—which I think is coming to an end, I hope creatively, although sometimes I fear, catastrophically—is that post-
Renaissance man, largely in his Western, maritime, post-
Christian incarnation, has tried his utmost to take no notice of either of these environments in his major activities.
If we look back over the past 400 years, we can see that the
chief drives, the chief aims and energies which have created the planet we live on now have in large measure acquired their force by almost totally neglecting the issue of
context, the context of both the moral and natural environment.* [6]

Whether we resolve these calamitous problems by harness-
ing our genius depends first of all on our willingness to re-
examine our ethics. In America that is difficult because the
business of America is *business*. Whatever ethics we choose,
therefore, from whatever set of presuppositions, must meet
criteria set by corporate interests. When Exxon Corporation
announces a 37 percent increase in profit margin, which figures out to $955 million in the first quarter, is that not an ethi-
cal issue? Is it not an environmental issue? Clearly it is both.

It is easy to pick on the oil companies, of course. Their
profits are so blatant, their impact on all of us so immediate.
What is more crucial is the philosophy operative in corporate
life in the U.S. and abroad. It is the assumption that the last,
best hope for humankind lies in the business sphere, that
what politicians, generals and hordes of preachers have
failed to produce, the business sector can bring about
through the expertise of entrepreneurs and managers; that
is, conditions conducive to human welfare. The ambition
is honorable. The problem, however, lies in the presup-
position on which the scheme is based: that human welfare
can best be served when persons with entrepreneurial gifts
are freed to be creatively self-centered. From that point of
view, Jesus was a nice man, but basically naive. It is the

selfish who will inherit the earth.

How can a system that glorifies selfishness respond bene-ficently to the ethical demand? Are there any built-in as-sumptions that might chart a new moral sensitivity? Will hope come from Harvard Business School? Can the "objec-tive laws of profit" provide enough "trickle" to guarantee more than subsistence for the world's needy? How do Chris-tians in such a system express themselves ethically?

It seems to me that the same dilemma faces the U.S. in the area of law. How does one insure justice in a society in which law loses its religious roots? Where does ethical perspective come from? If law is merely utilitarian or the sole province of the wealthy, how do we keep law from becoming a tool to insure order at the expense of justice?

That problem is especially crucial to those—especially black people—who have tenaciously supported the notion of a society under the rule of law rather than under rule by men. Today this historic confidence and support are eroding—the sentiment grows that Nixon has won after all, that Martin Luther King has lost to Allan Bakke. White college and semi-nary students are no longer as moved by ethics as they are by economics. Art Simon is more a prophet than the Berrigans.

THE THEOLOGICAL TASK
Our discussion takes place in a context shaped by the demand, built into the universe itself, that justice prevail in the human family. If it does not, the physical environment rebels. Add to this a certain, even narrow, eschatological perspective. Barbara Ward is not the only one to think that "the present period of history is coming to an end." From John Steinbeck to Hal Lindsay, from Billy Graham to the late U Thant, the fear has been expressed that time is running out on us. Ecologically, ethically, politically, morally, time is leaking out between our fingers—if not time, then for us in the West at least, moral initiative. And it is that loss that may

have the most telling effect on evangelism.

If as American evangelicals we have not found a way to translate our theology into ethical activity, so that the little people of the earth can discern our solidarity with them, then how much longer can we preach Christ with integrity? We have a major theological task yet to do and in my judgment it is primarily eschatological and Christological. It is eschatological in the sense that we must rescue the kingdom of God from the palsied hands of those who would have us believe that the apostle Paul's Christ is not Matthew's, or that the New Testament church has nothing to do with the Old Testament prophets. We must pray for eyes to see that even if the salvation of our God is intensely personal, it is never private; to see that salvation includes God's concern for nations as well. He is personal, but he is also political!

We need to work on our Christology also. We evangelicals insist that before we talk about style, we need to talk about life. We insist with evangelistic fervor that Jesus is the key to life, that he *is* life. But we need to ask Hans Küng's question: Which Jesus? The Jesus of the enthusiasts? The pietists? The revolutionists? Lifestyle must grow out of two primary perceptions if the wretched of the earth are to be served by shocked members of affluent societies. We must perceive who Christ really is and what is his total mission—not his primary mission, but his *total* mission.

This concern brings me back to Iran and that ancient dream. It is my growing conviction that the theme of the kingdom of God is the major unifying motif in the Scriptures. That theme captures the divine intention most fully. Within that frame of reference the people of God can most adequately deal with their total task in the earth, from evangelism to lifestyle to relief and justice. In that scheme Jesus is perceived not only as Savior but also and pre-eminently as Lord and King. In that role he commands his servants to proclaim the whole counsel of God and to wrap flesh around the words they profess. That is the only perspective capable of maintaining a creative tension between dogged activism and living hope. It is the one theme that unites the church in prayer and inspires prophetic servanthood: "Thy kingdom come ... on earth. ..."

Notes

[1]Economist Robert L. Heilbroner, author of *Between Capitalism and Socialism* (1970), *An Inquiry into the Human Prospect* (1974) and many other books.

[2]Ronald J. Sider, *Rich Christians in an Age of Hunger* (Downers Grove, Ill.: InterVarsity Press, 1977); Arthur Simon, *Bread for the World* (Grand Rapids, Mich., and Paramus, N. J.: Wm. B. Eerdmans and Paulist Press, 1975).

[3]"The Biblical Vision of the Ecological Crisis," *The Christian Century*, 22 November 1978, p. 1132.

[4]Lecture at Fuller Theological Seminary, 1978.

[5]Barbara Ward, "Justice in a Human Environment," *IDOC/International Documentation*, 53 (May 1973), p. 25.

[6]Ibid.

OLD TESTAMENT FOUNDATIONS FOR LIVING MORE SIMPLY

Frank E. Gaebelein

2

Some time ago a cartoon in *The New Yorker* showed a portly man and his wife looking through the picture window of their living room at a lovely vista of fields and trees. The man was saying: "God's country? Well, I suppose it is. But I own it."

There's a sense in which that cartoon points to what the U.S. Consultation on Simple Lifestyle is all about: the confusion between God's ownership of everything we have and our stewardship of it. The confusion is one we have all at some time slipped into, but would never think of expressing as crassly as the cartoonist did.

For me there's an element of confession in my participation here and, I suspect, for others also. I realize that I have much to learn about a simple lifestyle lived to the glory of

God. In one way or another, the culture we live in is pushing us toward more elaborate living. No society in history has been so incessantly stimulated as ours to spend more and more money on nonessentials. And if the resulting materialism hinders our witness to a needy world, as it surely does, all the fault by no means lies with Madison Avenue and its unremitting appeals to self-indulgence. It also lies with us. With all our devotion to the Bible, we evangelicals have not been biblical enough to resist the pressures around us. We are zealous for bringing people to Christ. (I say that without disparagement.) But we have neglected essential parts of Scripture in which God sets forth what he requires of us in our relationships to our neighbors. Our fault has been, and still is, an unbiblical selectivity in the preaching, reading and application of the Word of God.

Here is an excerpt from a full-page advertisement of a new Reference Bible: "At first glance you will recognize its major feature: a unique color shading system that instantly classifies all verses dealing with the four major Bible themes— Salvation, The Holy Spirit, Temporal Blessings, Prophecy." There you have in a nutshell the imbalance that is weakening evangelical obedience to the whole counsel of God.

Since the 1920s I have attended evangelical churches and participated in many Bible conferences. Yet never have I heard at a Bible conference a responsible treatment of the prophet Amos's strong words about injustices done through the misuse of wealth or an exposition of the great passages from Isaiah and other prophets that stress God's concern for the poor and oppressed. In fact, not till this year have I heard in a conservative evangelical church any really forthright preaching about these things, which are so important in God's sight. Prophecy, yes, but only in its predictive, eschatological aspects. Little or nothing is heard about the major witness of the prophets and other parts of the Old Testament against the idolatry of things and the oppression that may be entailed in accumulating them.

Why are many evangelicals apparently insensitive to injustice? One reason may be an Old Testament translation problem. A discussion with a Christian friend in Washington, a distinguished professional man, showed me that. We had been talking about civil rights and my friend amazed me by insisting that the Bible has practically nothing to say about justice. Like most older evangelicals, my friend was devoted to the King James Version. So I investigated the use of the word *justice* and found that in the KJV *mishpat*, the Hebrew word used far more than any other word for "justice," is translated "judgment" 294 times and "justice" only once. In over 90 of those 294 times, *mishpat* means "justice" and is so translated in newer versions. Thus for the reader of the KJV, Psalm 106:3, "Blessed are they who maintain justice" (NIV), is "Blessed are they that keep judgment"; Isaiah 30:18, "The Lord is a God of justice," is "The Lord is a God of judgment"; and Amos's magnificent imperative, "Let justice roll down like waters" (5:24), is narrowed to "Let judgment run down as waters." The same is true in scores and scores of passages.[1] Obviously, the KJV use of "judgment" for "justice" has for many readers obscured the totality of the Old Testament emphasis on justice, an emphasis vitally linked to the need for a simple lifestyle.

My subject requires me to deal with some Old Testament aspects of the question. If I may respectfully modify the title of a well-known book, let me ask, "How in this Affluent Society Should We then Live?" In reply I invite you to join me in looking at six categories of Old Testament teaching that shed light on the need for simplifying the way we are living. Here they are in the approximate order of their biblical occurrence:

1. The account of our creation
2. The decalogue
3. The sabbath year and the year of Jubilee

4. The tithe and the law of gleaning
5. The Shema: Deuteronomy 6:4-5
6. The general Old Testament teaching about wealth and possessions

THE ACCOUNT OF OUR CREATION: GENESIS 1 AND 2
In the account of our creation, "God said, 'Let us make man in our image, in our likeness, and let them rule over the fish of the sea and the birds of the air, over the livestock, over all the earth, and over all the creatures that move along the ground.' So God created man in his own image, in the image of God he created him; male and female, he created them" (Gen. 1:26-27 NIV).

That is positively the greatest thing ever said of humanity: God made us in his image, an image that, though marred through the Fall beyond human power to repair, is not beyond God's regenerating power. It is an image that has never been totally effaced. That is the source of human dignity—not wealth or position, but our creation in God's image. No one has put the implications of this more powerfully that C. S. Lewis in his sermon, "The Weight of Glory":

> *The dullest and most uninteresting person you talk to may one day be a creature which, if you saw it now, you would be strongly tempted to worship, or else a horror and a corruption such as you now meet, if at all, only in a nightmare.... You have never talked to a mere mortal. Nations, cultures, arts, civilizations [and, may I interpose, all the trappings of affluence]–these are mortal, and their life is to ours as the life of a gnat. But it is immortals whom we joke with, work with, marry, snub, and exploit–immortal horrors or everlasting splendours."*[2]

What has that to do with our subject? For one thing it sets our lifestyle in the perspective of the human dignity inherent in our creation. It compels us to see whether anything in the way we live tends to diminish or degrade the humanity of our fellow image-bearers. It forces us to grapple with the relation of our lifestyle to the needs of the poor and hungry and oppressed—those whom God himself is especially concerned about. The Old Testament makes it clear that God's people were to enjoy the fruit of the land and celebrate his goodness in joyful feasts. Yet along with that there had to be continuing provision for the needs of the poor and the hungry. Christians can do no less.

The account of our creation also gives us another perspective. In Genesis 1 is the first biblical reference to stewardship. God made human beings responsible for the earth: to "fill [it] and subdue it" and "rule over" all living things (Gen. 1:28 NIV). God put the man in the garden "to work it and take care of it" (Gen. 2:15 NIV). So humankind received a delegated authority, a subordinate administration for which they were accountable to God. The biblical principle of the relation of humanity to God's world is not ownership but stewardship. Therefore, for us to degrade the environment in the pursuit of affluence is to sin against our fellow image-bearers, because degrading the environment diminishes their rightful heritage. We who live in the most wasteful society in the world, which is consuming God-given natural resources at an unparalleled rate, must take that perspective seriously.

THE DECALOGUE: EXODUS 20:1-17

The first two commandments—against false gods, "You shall have no other gods before me" and against idolatry, "You shall not make for yourself an idol. . . . You shall not bow down to them or worship them" (NIV)—confront us with a basic perspective. The Old Testament refers many times, and not always negatively, to prosperity and riches. Yet it also insistently warns against the idolatry of material things and against allowing them to turn our hearts from God. In a sense the biblical history of Israel is one long record of their lapsing and of God's judgment upon them. What hap-

pened to Solomon, who began by asking God for wisdom
instead of wealth and ended up by letting his lifestyle betray
him into idolatry, including even the worship of Molech
(1 Kings 11:7), shows the inherent snare of affluence.

Not all idols are religious ones. Materialism, with its
inordinate preoccupation with money and things, is idolatrous. The mention of Molech, to whom human beings were
sacrificed, raises a question about the place of the automobile
in American life with its mounting toll of over 50,000
highway deaths[3]—a number that most Christians, including
those committed to social action, accept with little or no
protest. Surely a responsible Christian lifestyle must be
concerned about such a sore spot in our national life and
reckon with the idolatrous pride of possession that so often
goes with car ownership.

Consider next the fourth commandment. In their reaction
against sabbatarian legalism most evangelicals have given
little thought to the sabbath principle in the Old Testament. It
is true that Christians are not bound by the Hebrew sabbath
regulations in their keeping of the Lord's Day. Nevertheless,
the sabbath has important things to say to us. One of them
relates to the desire to acquire things, a desire that coexists
with affluence in a kind of symbiotic relationship. Dr. Joshua
O. Haberman, senior rabbi of the Washington Hebrew Congregation, gave me this perspective on the fourth commandment when I told him about my assignment for this consultation: "On the Sabbath," he said, "I must acknowledge God the
Creator by resting from my acquisitiveness, because I have no
real title to anything. The Sabbath is the day that fully shows
God as Creator. In it we add nothing to what he has done. For
the first time in history the Sabbath brought a cessation from
human acquisitiveness."

One of the pitfalls of a lifestyle marked by acquisition of
more and more things of all kinds, irrespective of need, is the
false sense of ownership it fosters. But the sabbath reminds us

of our creatureliness in its witness to God as Creator and to his ownership of everything including material wealth (in Old Testament terms, "the cattle on a thousand hills," "the silver and the gold," "the earth . . . and the fulness thereof").

Look now at the tenth commandment. Consider the actual link between its prohibition of covetousness and the Fall in Eden. It was covetousness, the inordinate desire for unpossessed good, that the serpent used to entice Adam and Eve into rebelling against God. The temptation was for them to reach out for another lifestyle that was not God's will for them. So the tenth commandment probes the sin behind the progressive aggrandizement that leads Christians in our materialistic society into idolatrous lifestyles in which almost everything is spent on self and only a pittance is given to help the poor and hungry. Inherent in covetousness is idolatry. The New Testament word for covetousness (pleonexia) has the meaning of "wanting more and more," and Paul was right in saying twice (Eph. 5:5; Col. 3:5) that covetousness (greed, NIV) is idolatry. So an increasingly elaborate lifestyle, spurred by constant pressures to keep on getting things, comes full circle with the first two commandments.

THE SABBATH YEAR AND THE YEAR OF JUBILEE: LEVITICUS 25

Few Old Testament passages have been more closely studied by socially concerned Christians than Leviticus 25. In it the sabbath principle of the fourth commandment is extended and intensified. As Hans Ruedi-Weber says, "You cannot understand the Jubilee Year without understanding the Sabbath." Built into the Jubilee year regulations is the principle that the land does not belong to us but to God. We are "strangers and sojourners" (aliens and tenants, NIV) in it. Coupled with that are some powerful economic perspectives. As Arthur Holmes said in The Reformed Journal, the Jubilee year regulations "prevented the perpetuation of destitution by periodically returning to the family those lands which had passed into the possession of others. The veto on Israelites charging [interest] is not in itself unjust. Fair pricing was also required, a corollary of the fact that business is a service to others rather than the pursuit of unqualified self-interest."[4]

But liberation was also built into the Jubilee year. In that year the slaves were to be freed, a provision that was likewise built into the sabbath year. Since it was only the prosperous Israelites who had slaves, that was an act of justice for the poor. Nor should we think that the provisions about slaves are irrelevant for us. All oppression of others is a form of bondage, and lifestyles that lord it over others are tainted with the spirit of slavery.

One more point: The time when the Jubilee year was proclaimed throughout the land was the tenth day of the seventh month, the day of atonement. So its context in Israel's calendar was one of reconciliation. With its check on unrestrained aggrandizement and its stress on rectifying injustices the Jubilee year gives us perspectives on the relation between the way we use our resources (of which the land and slaves in Old Testament times were the counterpart) and the reconciliation available to us all in Christ—rich and poor alike. In short, the link of the Jubilee year with the day of atonement reinforces the principle that we must not tolerate anything in our lifestyle that will diminish our brother or sister for whom Christ died.

THE TITHE AND THE LAW OF GLEANING

Four principal Old Testament passages set forth the law of tithing in Israel: Leviticus 27:30-33; Numbers 18:21-32; Deuteronomy 12:5-18; Deuteronomy 14:22-29. Questions as to how many tithes there were are for scholars to answer, but the perspectives of Old Testament tithing are plain. The practice of setting aside one-tenth of all produce of the land including that derived from the animals that subsisted on it powerfully affirmed stewardship. Tithing clearly implied that everything humanity has belongs to God. Imbedded in its laws was the compassionate provision that at the end of every third year the tithe for that year was to be laid up for the use of the Levites, and that the fatherless and widows were to come and eat it. So a kind of reserve would be built up.

Akin to that was the law of gleaning (Lev. 19:9-10; Deut. 24:19-21). It required that at the harvest the fields were not to be reaped to their very borders nor the vineyards or olive groves stripped bare. Something was always to be left for the poor and the sojourners. (The second chapter of Ruth gives us a poignant picture of that practice.) We see, then, that in the "law of gleaning" God put into the economy of Israel still another compassionate requirement for helping the needy. That divine concern should lead us rich Christians to reassess the extent to which we are sharing our resources with the poor.

THE SHEMA: DEUTERONOMY 6:4-5

"Hear, O Israel: The LORD our God is one LORD; and you shall love the LORD your God with all your heart, and with all your soul, and with all your might." In those words, part of what in the Hebrew liturgy is called the *Shema*, a confession of faith, is followed by an exhortation. The pattern is, as John Stott says in his exposition of the section in the Lausanne Covenant on Christian social responsibilities, that "our theology must always govern our conduct." For us the perspectives implicit in those words in Deuteronomy are especially important, because the Lord Jesus used them, along with Leviticus 19:18, in defining the heart of Christian obedience based on love: "You shall love the Lord your God with all your heart, and with all your soul, and with all your mind. This is the great and first commandment. And a second is like it, You shall love your neighbor as yourself. On these two commandments depend all the law and the prophets" (Mt. 22:37-40).

Central to the *Shema* is the exhortation to love God, which occurs in Deuteronomy and nowhere else in the Old Testament. Without question, the three terms—with all your heart, soul and might—include our total being, our mind and will and desires, our emotions, our intellectual and physical energies.[5] Yes, and our possessions too. The Jewish commentator Rashi related the words "with all your might" to "with all your money, for," he said, "you sometimes find a man whose money is dearer to him than his life." Inevitably Deuteronomy 6:4-5 probes the integrity of our commitment to the God who "did not spare his own Son, but gave him up for us all" (Rom. 8:32 NIV). From this perspective we must examine our lifestyles to find the extent to which they reflect our love for God and our love for our neighbor. Hard questions come to mind: Does an indulgent lifestyle betray a failure in love? Is increasing expenditure on material things depriving our poor and hungry neighbors of help? Is idolatry of things imparing the integrity of our love for God?

Look at the context of that great declaration in Deuteronomy 6:4. Verses 6 and 7 take us straight to the home: "These words which I command you this day shall be upon your heart; and you shall teach them diligently to your children, and shall talk of them when you sit in your house, and when you walk by the way, and when you lie down and when you rise." There you see the principle, so often obscured today when both parents work to support more affluent living, that the home is the greatest educational force there is. Deuteronomy 6:6-7 compels us to think about what our lifestyle is teaching our children. Does it make them feel entitled to more and more things, a feeling which characterizes children of the affluent?[6] Does it show them that, beyond our oral testimony, we love God with our whole being, with our money too, and that we love our neighbor as ourselves?

THE GENERAL TEACHING ABOUT WEALTH AND POSSESSIONS

The Old Testament says much about wealth and possessions. Passage after passage deals with those subjects. Scripture neither idealizes poverty nor condemns wealth and prosperity as themselves evil. In his covenant-dealings with his people, God rewards obedience with material prosperity. There are Scripture promises—not a few of them—of temporal blessings for God's people. But along with them, there is always the underlying premise of God's sole ownership of everything and of his grace in doing for his people what they cannot do for themselves. As Ronald Sider points out, though the Old Testament says that God gives prosperity to the righteous, it denies the opposite—namely, that wealth and prosperity always indicate righteousness. On the contrary, the Old Testament shows over and over that wealth may be the fruit of oppression and exploitation, sins for which God has not only destroyed individuals but wiped out whole nations.

"Trust in the LORD, and do good; so you will dwell in the land, and enjoy security. Take delight in the LORD, and he will give you the desires of your heart" (Ps. 37:3-4). Many thoughtful readers of the Old Testament have been faced with the tension between the promises of prosperity for the righteous and the plain fact that the righteous are sometimes poor and needy through no fault of their own. The writer of Psalm 37 apparently overlooked that circumstance when he wrote: "I have been young, and now am old; yet I have never seen the righteous forsaken or his children begging bread." Perhaps he was stating the norm to which there are always exceptions. It's interesting that when that psalm is read in Jewish worship after a meal the leader reads that particular verse silently lest a righteous poor person should hear it and be offended.

For a divine perspective on the tension we feel between

the righteous poor and the flourishing wicked, we may go to
Psalm 73. In that psalm, a person named Asaph tells how
troubled he was. His feet had "almost slipped," he said,
when he saw the wicked. They were strong, proud and carefree, boasting in the enjoyment of their wealth. "When I tried
to understand all this," he wrote, "it was oppressive to me till
I entered the sanctuary of God; then I understood their final
destiny" (Ps. 73:16-17 NIV). There follows in the psalm the
picture of the swift destruction of the wicked rich as God's
inexorable judgment overtakes them.

The Old Testament sets wealth and prosperity in perspective. It hedges them about with restrictions and cautions.
Wealth is not to be accumulated just for the sake of getting
more and more, it must not be gained by oppression and injustice, it can and does lead to covetousness. Wealth does not
belong to us but to God, who is the ultimate owner of all we
have. We are stewards, not proprietors, of our wealth. In our
use of it, we are sinning if we do not reflect God's special
concern for the poor and hungry, the weak and oppressed.
What we do with what we have must be in accord with the
great command to love God with everything we are and have.
Even our ability to gain wealth is a stewardship like any
other talent. The Old Testament reminds us that it is God
who has given us the ability to get wealth: "Beware lest you
say in your heart, 'My power and the might of my hand have
gotten me this wealth.' You shall remember the LORD your
God, for it is he who gives you power to get wealth" (Deut.
8:17-18).

The Old Testament does not tell us specifically whether
we should buy a better car, keep the one we have or have no
car at all. It does not tell us whether we should upgrade our
lifestyle by getting a bigger house, or cut it back by getting a
smaller one. It doesn't specify exactly what our lifestyle
should be. Rather, it gives us certain principles by which we
must measure our lifestyle. To face those principles honestly

and prayerfully is bound to lead to changes that will help us simplify our lives in order to be more obedient disciples of our Lord.

Notes

[1]Though two other Hebrew words for "justice" (*tsedeq* and *tsedaqah*) are translated "justice" a total of 25 times in the KJV, that hardly offsets the loss occasioned by the KJV use of "judgment" where "justice" is meant.

[2](New York: Macmillan, 1949), p. 15.

[3]See "Traffic Deaths Surge Past 50,000," *The Washington Post*, 21 April 1979.

[4]October 1978.

[5]*Beacon Bible Commentary* (Kansas City, Mo.: Beacon Hill Press, n.d.), I, 536.

[6]See Robert Coles, "The Children of Affluence," *Atlantic Monthly*, September 1977.

NEW TESTAMENT FOUNDATIONS FOR LIVING MORE SIMPLY

Peter H. Davids

3

What does the New Testament say about lifestyle? Not much it seems. The New Testament is not concerned with lifestyle, but with new life in Christ. Lifestyle flows out of the basic perspective of the New Testament. We must first uncover the basic ethical perspectives of the New Testament and then observe how these unfold in its teaching on lifestyle.[1] We begin, then, by asserting that New Testament ethics are (1) Christocentric, (2) eschatological, (3) charismatic and (4) communal.

Christocentric means that Christ and the present lordship of Christ are axiomatic for the new community. Christ is the authoritative teacher who gives the key for Old Testament reinterpretation, who presents a new ethic for a new age, who lived that ethic before his disciples and who died to free them for that new life. He is also the resurrected Lord to whom the church submits and who still speaks through the prophets. "Jesus is Lord" is not a credal formula, but a slogan for a way of life in submission to Christ.[2]

The term *eschatological* refers to the New Testament axiom that these are the last days, that we live in the tension between the inauguration and consummation of the end times. Since Christians live under the belief that the present age is drawing to a close (i.e., Christ will return), they can live as if the future age were already here, anticipating the future reward in their actions and the future unity in the church. If we reject the eschatology of the New Testament, we automatically join those who thereby reject the relevance of New Testament ethics.[3]

By *charismatic* we mean that the new age has brought the advent of the Spirit, who empowers the new life of the Christian community. Jesus taught in the power of the Spirit, and at Pentecost that power was released into the wider Christian community, forming it into a true people of God. The Spirit produced evangelism, miracles and the sharing of goods; all are essential to authentic experience like theirs. But more important, the dynamic of the Spirit means that the new ethic flows from *within* in response to the reception of God's "wisdom"; it is not imposed from without (such attempts result in legalism, ideology or "guilt trips" and are unable to transform individuals).[4]

Finally, the term *communal* means that the focus of New Testament ethics is the new community welded together by allegiance to Christ and the presence of the Spirit. That eschatological community provides not only the focal point but also the supportive relationships necessary to live out the new life. Thus the "new person" is indeed a person-in-community with an ethic which is not so much a *Konventikelethik* as a church-ethic.

Obviously these perspectives make the ethic of the New

Testament "nonsense" to those who are not devoted to the
Christ on whom it centers. The world lacks the wisdom of
God and thus must reject or rationalize the ethic to make it
"realistic" within its own context. Those within the church
often share the same problem, for our minds have been partly
captured by the thought-forms of the world. Thus to avoid
distortion we must always call ourselves back to the basic
perspectives.

JESUS

With those perspectives, we turn to the teaching of Jesus. He
must be the center and origin of any ethic pretending to be
Christian.

The most conspicuous part of the teaching of Jesus is his
demand for radical commitment to the kingdom of God. The
call of the kingdom demands the greatest sacrifice, spurns
halfhearted commitment and overrides the most sacred
duties (Mt. 13:44-46; Lk. 9:57-62). The commitment is one of
total trust in which such mundane matters as food and clothing are left to God while we devote ourselves to the kingdom
(Mt. 6:33; 7:7-12). Thus Jesus' teaching is never "practical"
in the ordinary sense of the word, for it is based on an impractical commitment, a total trust in a new world order and its
Ruler, for whom we must be prepared to suffer and die (see
Mt. 10).

Lifestyle, then, is viewed from the perspective of the kingdom. The narrative of the rich young ruler will give us the
best foothold (Mk. 10:17-31; Mt. 19:16-30; Lk. 18: 18-30). A
young man comes to Jesus seeking eternal life.[5] Two important questions are asked of him: Has he recognized the lordship of God in obeying God's revealed will? Does he know
that "obedience to God must be demonstrated by acknowl-
edging that God meets us in Jesus"?[6] The first question is
quickly disposed of: "Teacher, all these I have observed from
my youth" (Mk. 10:20). He was a person who, like the apostle

Paul, could claim to have been faithful to the Law (see Phil. 3:6), and Jesus accepts his claim. The second question, however, is so stated that Jesus loses a potential convert. Jesus makes the sale of his goods a condition of discipleship. The man is rich and cannot make that sacrifice. He departs. Then Jesus compounds our consternation by generalizing the demand beyond the single case (Mk. 10:23-25). No wonder the disciples were astonished.

In explaining that passage most Christians shy away from its implications. We tend to agree with Clement of Alexandria that the important part is *attitude* toward wealth, not the giving up of wealth per se.[7] Can there be a true inward attitude without outward consequences? Is it not hypocrisy to teach one way and live another? One might suggest that the point is not wealth at all; rather, we must renounce anything that comes between us and God.[8] Although it is true that Mark 10:24 does broaden the application beyond the wealthy and Mark 10:28-31 applies the giving up to more than possessions, the fact remains that the narrative focuses on wealth and the explanation twice returns to the wealthy (Mk. 10:23, 25). We conclude that Jesus indicates two uncomfortable facts: His followers must in life as well as in attitude be detached from all that keeps them from total commitment, and wealth is one of the greatest barriers to that commitment, perhaps the greatest.

Jesus, of course, was no ascetic. Even though he did fast at least once and was relatively poor himself, he glorified neither poverty nor abstention from pleasure. On the contrary, he was known as a "drunkard and a glutton," a "friend of tax-gatherers and sinners," who "ate with them." Luke in particular often presents Jesus at a meal; his disciples were criticized for not fasting. For him good things were to be enjoyed, but his conduct showed that he had no investment in them. They were not essential to his lifestyle. Thus he could wander with a band of disciples whose only guarantee

of support was "the Father in heaven," living out the teaching of trust presented in Matthew 6:25-34. His life was no
search for holy poverty, but rather a joyful acceptance of both
poverty and abundance as the will of his Father.

Yet wealth was hardly a thing indifferent to Jesus. Serving
it cuts one off from God. The very word, *mammon*, indicates
evil character (Mt. 6:24).[9] Those who keep their money, no
matter how honestly it is earned, are consistently con-
demned by Jesus (Lk. 12:13-21; 16:19-31). The disciples are
praised because they gave up their security in this world
(Mk. 10:28-31). Zacchaeus is declared saved after he parts
with not only his illegitimate gain, but half of all his wealth.
Likewise John the Baptist demands sharing as a prerequisite
for repentance (Lk. 3:10-14). The reason for rejection of
wealth is that wealth roots us in the wrong place, that is, on
earth (Lk. 12:34). Luke records that the Son of man came to
give his life. For our sake, the apostle Paul writes, he held on
to nothing of his own (Phil. 2:6-11). That means that any radical commitment to Christ will result in a lifestyle of giving as
well. Giving and hoarding are mutually exclusive options.

Three themes in the teaching of Jesus bring out that fact.
First, the Old Testament taught the love of neighbor (in imitation of God), but Jesus radicalized the giving implicit in
that command: in the Good Samaritan parable he commands
us to copy a man who risked both life and fortune for the sake
of an unknown member of an unfriendly nation (Lk. 10:25-
37). Giving for Jesus goes to the point of personal risk.

Second, the teaching of Jesus, especially in the form recorded by Luke,[10] stresses God's special concern for the poor.
That concern is seen whether one looks at the Magnificat
with its reversal of the roles of rich and poor, at Jesus' reference to preaching the gospel to the poor as the climactic
evidence of the arrival of the Messiah (Mt. 11:5; Lk. 4:18-19;
7:22; cf. Is. 61:1), at his command to invite the poor to our
feasts (Lk. 14), or at the beatitudes, whose "Poor in spirit" are

surely to be thought of as the pious, oppressed people mentioned so frequently in the later Old Testament Scriptures and the intertestamental literature.[11] God does care about the poor.

Third, Jesus specifically commands the sharing of resources. Beginning with the beatitudes one notes that those who give to the poor (the "merciful"),[12] those single-mindedly devoted to God ("pure in heart"), those making peace (an important form of social righteousness) and those suffering in producing righteousness are all pronounced blessed. One can go further, noting that the parables of the rich man and Lazarus and of the rich fool both imply that giving the surplus away would have been the right thing to do. Finally one has the clear commands (Mt. 6:19-34), beginning with a direct command to put one's treasure in heaven. The rest of the passage works out that theme (having a single, i.e., generous, "eye"; living freely as the birds; etc.). The meaning of putting treasure in heaven is clearly spelled out for us in gentile language in Luke's reaction: "Sell your possessions, and give alms; provide yourselves with purses that do not grow old, with a treasure in the heavens that does not fail, where no thief approaches and no moth destroys. For where your treasure is, there will your heart be also" (Lk. 12:33-34).

The command is unavoidable: Jesus loved and therefore gave; we are also to love and therefore give. The hand that remains closed in the face of need reveals a heart totally ignorant of Jesus, a life in which Jesus is anything but Lord.

THE EARLY CHURCH

As the charismatic eschatological community the early church worked out in practice the commands of its risen Lord. Although we must be aware that in Acts at least we are dealing with descriptive and not necessarily normative material, we have grounds for believing that Luke presents the descriptions in Acts not simply as local ideals, but also as descriptions of what to some extent all churches he knew were like.[13]

The two main summary passages (Acts 2:43-47; 4:32—5:11) exhibit three dynamic forces which describe the Christian lifestyle: (1) single-minded commitment to God demonstrated in the frequent prayers and gatherings; (2) experience of the presence of God revealed in the activity of the Holy Spirit (notice that each summary follows a filling of the Spirit); and (3) deep concern for one another (koinonia) indicated by the sharing of goods and meals.

It is sometimes wrongly assumed that the communal sharing ("they had all things in common," 2:44) indicates a total rejection of private ownership. The texts point to a somewhat different situation. There was certainly a subjective release from a need for private possession, for "no one said that any of the things which he possessed was his own" (4:32). But the objective divestiture and redistribution of goods in both passages was a process which took place gradually according to the needs of the community.[14] Sharing was not a rule to be followed but a result of deep spirituality, of mutual love and care. Barnabas forms Luke's positive example of the process and Ananias and Sapphira an example of abuse.

Further passages in Acts work out the procedure for fair distribution (6:1-6), describe the need for interchurch as well as intrachurch aid (11:27-30) and point to the fact that Paul subordinated his own economic interests to the good of the church (20:33-35). The sharing which Jesus commanded, then, is described by Luke in Acts as an illustration of the love which has transformed the lives of Christians and enabled them to fulfill the hope of the Old Testament.[15]

The catholic epistles, which reflect an early paraenetic (exhortatory) tradition, give a similar picture of the church. In James, for instance, the rich are not to trust in their buying and selling, but to do good (Jas. 4:13-17; the "good" is probably charity) and boast in their being brought low (1:10-11). Christians must remember that faith needs works, which are primarily the aiding of the poor (1:26-27). In fact, without such works of charity as Abraham and Rahab showed, any claim to faith is useless. Works-less people are as hell-bound as the demons (2: 14-26). It is therefore important to keep free of the world, particularly mammon, for such entanglements make one God's enemy (Jas. 4:1-8; compare the "strangers and pilgrims" language of 1 Peter and the "love not the world" concept of 1 John). James, then, repeats Jesus' black-and-white language. One either follows the way of love or else demonstrates that he or she is outside the faith. (John, in 1 Jn. 3:11-18, repeats that idea, and in 1 Jn. 4:7-12 he denies that those who do not demonstrate love-in-action even know God.)[16] The above picture meshes well with the examples given in Acts: the teaching in the catholic epistles (undoubtedly illumined by the "wisdom from above" as James would say, or by the Spirit as John would say) encouraged early believers in the practices described in Acts.

PAUL

The intense loyalty to Jesus' teachings seen in both Acts and the catholic epistles is also shown by the apostle Paul. The Damascus road experience left an indelible mark on Paul. Christ was the origin and center of his reoriented life; the Holy Spirit was his dynamic; the power of life had replaced the power of death, as Paul argued in Romans 8. The Spirit's power enables the Christian to live up to the glorious calling of following Christ, which means in practice, "whether you eat or drink, or whatever you do, do all to the glory of God. Give no offense to Jews or to Greeks or to the church of God, just as I try to please all men in everything I do, not seeking my own advantage, but that of many, that they may be saved. Be imitators of me, as I am of Christ" (1 Cor. 10:31 —11:1).

That is Paul's lifestyle in a nutshell. Its goal is the glory of

God (a Pharasaic and Old Testament theme), but its means is the *imitatio Christi*.[17] The pattern of Christ is used to judge every action. In each issue Paul asks: How does this allow one to copy Christ? How does this contribute to the work Christ is doing? How does this build his body on earth? For example, Paul applies such considerations to questions of marriage versus celibacy, of eating idol sacrifices and of accepting remuneration for ministerial services (1 Cor. 7-10). No part of one's lifestyle is unimportant; everything comes under the same rule.

Given the above as axiomatic, what are some of the basic parameters of that kind of lifestyle? First, just as Jesus distrusted wealth, and in continuity with his eschatological hope, Paul viewed the Christian way of life as being in radical discontinuity with that of the world. "The world," which would include all political systems, ideologies, social values or ethical formulations of this age, is an enemy, subverting us from total conformity to Christ (Rom. 12:1-2). It represents a now alien force which once held us in bondage, under the control of "the prince of the power of the air," but its time has come to an end: "I mean, brethren, the appointed time has grown very short; from now on, let those who have wives live as though they had none, and those who mourn as though they were not mourning, and those who rejoice as though they were not rejoicing, and those who buy as though they had no goods, and those who deal with the world as though they had no dealings with it. For the form of this world is passing away" (1 Cor. 7:29-31).

That means that the Christian lifestyle must ignore the "realities" of this present age, for no matter how firmly entrenched they may seem to be they are coming to an end. The Christian is to live out the already-present and soon-coming new age, demonstrating the reconciliation which Christ has produced in the world (Eph. 2:14-22) within the new community, the church (which is collectively subject to and patterned after Christ—Eph. 1:22).

Second, since the pattern of Christ was one of a suffering servant (see Phil. 2:6-11), Paul's lifestyle is one of suffering for others in specific life situations. That suffering is so real collectively and individually that in bearing the pains of others one shares the suffering of Christ (Col. 1:24; 2 Cor. 1:5-6). For Paul that meant working long hours to support his ministry, giving up his right to financial support and risking the dangers of travel. Paul counsels Christians similarly: subordinate your financial interests to the cause of Christ, so that you would rather suffer financial loss than take another Christian to court (1 Cor. 6:1-11); subordinate yourselves to each other in personal, familial and social relations.[18] That pattern of life totally rejects the normal values of society, especially those of claiming one's own rights.

Third, Paul, like Jesus, was suspicious of wealth unless it was being used in good works. It is not that Paul was ascetic; he evidently had no pangs of conscience about enjoying a good meal or the hospitality of wealthy Christians. He knew how to abound (Phil. 4:10-14), but like Jesus he had no attachment to such comforts—he also knew how to be abased. Good things were enjoyed, but not grasped. He freely shared what he had and taught that one should be content with food and clothing alone. "Those who desire to be rich fall into temptation, into a snare, into many senseless and hurtful desires" (1 Tim. 6:9-10). Therefore some of the chief vices Paul condemns are greediness, self-seeking and cupidity.[19] "The love of money is the root of all evils." Wealth tends to entangle us in the world's system and lead us away from the suffering generosity of Christ.

Naturally, Paul was not ignorant of the fact that some Christians did have surpluses. He had clear directions for them. Earning more than one needs is good, but that is because one can then share (Eph. 4:28). All who have more than enough must so reorient their priorities that they become rich in good works. They must put their treasure in heaven by sharing it with poorer believers (1 Tim. 6:17-19). These, of course, must have included not only childless widows and the elders of the community (1 Tim. 5:1-18), but also other needy Christians. Otherwise it would be hard to explain the abuses Paul combats.[20]

Sharing also extended beyond the boundaries of the local church. Christ's body was one, so any suffering church must be helped as much as possible. In that respect Paul's aid for the Jerusalem church is paradigmatic.[21] He makes clear in 2 Corinthians 8-9 that such aid must be voluntary, coming from a previous commitment to Christ and the inner impulse of the Spirit. Because it must be a joyful response to God in the light of need, Paul cannot talk about "fair shares" or place a levy on the church. On the other hand, he has certain fundamental principles in mind which indicate that churches should, under the guidance of the Spirit, share economic and other resources on the basis of equality: "I do not mean that others should be eased and you burdened, but that as a matter of equality your abundance at the present time should supply their want, so that their abundance may supply your want, that there may be equality. As it is written, 'He who gathered much had nothing over, and he who gathered little had no lack' " (2 Cor. 8:13-15).

In announcing that Christians ought to live as part of a transracial, transnational community of sharing, Paul declares a radical principle about lifestyle. For him the imitation of Christ (explicitly cited in those chapters) and the loving care of Christians know no limits. Paul rejoices to see poor Macedonians sacrificing in their poverty to assist still-poorer Jerusalem Christians.[22]

CONCLUDING THOUGHTS

Having surveyed the biblical data, we can now draw together some interpretations of what sort of lifestyle could be called biblical in light of New Testament theology. I intend only to be suggestive at this point. Our interpretations like our survey must be brief, without going into the question of hermeneutics. Perhaps the following theses will form a basis for reflection.

1. The thesis that all Christian lifestyles must be Christocentric, eschatological, charismatic and communal has been demonstrated throughout the New Testament in all genres of its literature. There must be a prior commitment to Christ with a concomitant renunciation of self. There must be an eschatological expectation with an ability to accept present suffering. There must be an inner dynamic of the Spirit with an ability to change the heart. There must be a new community with supportive functions before a truly biblical lifestyle can become a lasting reality—without either burning itself out or lapsing into a new legalism.

2. A biblical lifestyle will necessarily recognize itself as being in opposition to the prevailing values and lifestyle of its culture. It is informed by a different view of reality. God calls "blessed" whom the world calls "miserable," and "miserable" whom the world calls "blessed." The world, lying in darkness, cannot understand the light of Christ, cannot comprehend that a poor weak church is ultimately more powerful than its mightiest empires, weapons and strategies. Therefore the Christian community must be on its guard against being co-opted by the world on the one hand and succumbing to triumphalism on the other. The church may appear to win as the world adopts some aspects of the Christian lifestyle, but there is no hope that the world as a whole will ever willingly adopt Christ's values. Although the church must reach out to the world, its ultimate hope is in the eschaton (the final consummation). When the church thinks that it is triumphing and becoming influential, it probably behooves the church to ask if the world has not succeeded in domesticating it.

3. A biblical lifestyle will be based on the *imitatio Christi*.
Christ is the head, the lord of the Christian, the master
teacher, the pathfinder, the example. Such imitation, of
course, is a form of the *imitatio dei*, since Jesus called us to be
imitators of God (Mt. 5:48). Primarily that imitation will
mean following the pattern of the love of the enemy in suffering service. The Christian lifestyle will be reconciling and
peacemaking (Mt. 5:9, Jas. 3:17-18), which was the activity of
Christ. Our simplicity should include no room for hostility,
bitterness and war. Such a lifestyle will therefore include
giving and suffering; the world (which cannot understand
reconciliation) will bring us suffering, and the needs of
others will call for giving.

4. The primary focus of the Christian lifestyle will be the
worldwide Christian community. This principle does not
mean that Christians are to have no interest in the poor who
do not share their faith. The parable of the good Samaritan,
the command to do good to all (Gal. 6:10) and the example of
Jesus show otherwise. Rather this principle means that
Christians are *especially* concerned about our brothers and
sisters, partially because some of their suffering is a result of
their faith, yet also because our display of solidarity is obedience to the command of Christ (Jn. 13:34-35). Also, it is
only within the community of faith that a living demonstration of the new order can be set up. The New Testament has
very little information about how we might assist the world,
but plenty of details about how our lifestyle should affect
other believers.[23]

5. A biblical lifestyle will be suspicious of wealth. Wealth
means success on worldly terms, which raises the question
of how it was obtained and why it is maintained. Certainly
the church dares have no preference for or emulation of the
wealthy (see Jas. 2:1-13). In fact, the very idea of some people
living well on their store of goods while others suffer should
be abhorrent. But suspicion of wealth must mean neither a

judgmental attitude nor personal rejection. It will mean instead praising and honoring those whose wealth is matched by their liberality. It will also mean self-examination to see where we, whatever our economic status, have put our security in this world. Our security rests not in preserving our luxuries in the face of others' wants, nor in worshiping mammon, nor in clinging to life itself.

6. A biblical lifestyle will be one of sharing with and caring for others. That means emulating God's concern for the poor, recognizing that we meet Christ in suffering (Mt. 25:31-46), and desiring to simplify our lifestyle. We examine our wants to see if they are luxuries; we examine our needs to see if they are actually culturally mandated wants. Such self-examination should free more of our resources to share with others. Obedience to Christ's command to "sell and give" focuses first on our neighbor's needs, but must include the worldwide community of faith. No Christian should rest comfortably with his or her lifestyle so long as it allows life with surplus while a brother or sister somewhere in the world is suffering relievable want. Christians should also examine our lifestyle, especially our economic practices, to see if they are contributing to the injury of some brother or sister in another part of the worldwide economy. Both relief and the prevention of harm through changed economic practices fit under the rubric of care and love.

7. A biblical lifestyle will always stress *moderation*. Even where others are neither damaged by our consumption nor able to be relieved by our abstinence and sharing, we must count excess bad. New Testament vice lists point to drunkenness, gluttony and expensive clothing right alongside murder, homosexuality and adultery.[24] All people are to see our moderation, says Paul (Phil. 4:5). Christians may indulge in moderation (in proper food or in sex within marriage), but they also abstain.[25] The ability to use without abusing, to accept within limits, demonstrates our freedom from the

world. Although we enjoy the physical world as God's creation, our true inheritance lies in a new creation.

In pointing to the pattern of Christ, to love, to sharing and
to moderation, we have pointed to the freedom of the Christian in biblical theology. The Christian lifestyle is a simple
lifestyle. It gives instead of hoarding and limits instead of
consumes. But it is not a lifestyle of *must*: it is one of "you
can," "you are no longer bound to," "you are free to." Thus
the Christian lifestyle is celebration, for the New Testament
presents it as the freedom of the Spirit. The greatness and the
severity of the demand is matched only by the power of the
One who calls us to it.

Notes

[1]This paper is essentially a revision and condensation of an earlier work,
"God and Mammon: The Bible and Christian Lifestyle," published in
the March and April issues of *Sojourners*, 1978, and forthcoming from
Shaftesbury Project as a pamphlet. This was in turn dependent on earlier
articles in *Incite*, the *Post American*, and *Themelios* as well as my dis-
sertation. Each revision has impressed on me more the need to push back
to the theological roots before attempting ethical discussion.

[2]The new rule of life for the early church was embodied in the paraenetic
(exhortatory) tradition which we have received in the new law of the
Sermon on the Mount and in the exposited versions of James, Paul and
John.

[3]For example, see Jack T. Sanders, *Ethics in the New Testament* (Philadelphia: Fortress Press, 1975) or J. L. Houlden, *Ethics and the New Testament* (Oxford: Oxford Univ. Press, 1977). Both draw the conclusion
that since we do not expect the coming of Christ as the early church did,
its ethic is irrelevant for us.

[4]Both Peter's response to Ananias in Acts 5 and Paul's argument in 2 Corinthians 8-9 underline this issue. While the generous response is
lauded, there is no attempt to establish a rule or impose generosity. The
activity of the Spirit is recognized in the joyful response to need, with
rules serving mainly to keep one from identifying false impulses with
those of the Spirit. Cf. note 17 below.

[5]He is seeking salvation, not a special place among the disciples. See E.
Schweizer, *The Good News According to Mark* (London: SPCK, 1971),

p. 210; T. W. Manson, *The Teaching of Jesus* (Cambridge: Cambridge Univ. Press, 1931), p. 206; and V. Taylor, *The Gospel According to Mark* (London: Macmillan, 1952), p. 429.

[6]Schweizer, p. 212.

[7]*Quis dives salvetur.* A step in the direction of making the renunciation purely inward (and so making the church more comfortable for the wealthy) is found in the more radical *Shepherd of Hermas.* The present essay does not have space to discuss the position of the early church fathers, but see M. Hengel, *Property and Riches in the Early Church* (Philadelphia: Fortress Press, 1974), who discusses both the New Testament and the first few hundred years of the church.

[8]Schweizer, pp. 212-213.

[9]Luke clarified that connotation for his gentile readers by calling it "unrighteous mammon." In our judgment Jesus is drawing from the stream of Judaism in his day in which wealth indicated unrighteousness. See, for example, 1 Enoch 63:10, 94-105, and 108:7, F. Hauck notices that fact in his article, 'mamonas' in vol. IV of *Theological Dictionary of the New Testament* (ed. G. Kittel [Grand Rapids, Mich.: Eerdmans, 1967], pp. 389-390), stating, "This realistic view of the actual facts makes it impossible for Jesus to think of earthly possessions with religious optimism or to regard them as a mark of special divine blessing."

[10]It has long been recognized that Luke has a special interest in the poor. H. J. Degenhardt, for example, wrote a book on that theme *(Lukas: Evangelist der Armen* [Stuttgart: Katholisches Bibelwerk, 1965]). It also forms a major part of J. Navone's *Themes of St. Luke* (Rome: Gregorian Univ. Press, 1970). Luke's interest means that he arranges the material which he has in common with Matthew so as to make this teaching more emphatic. The interest is found in Acts as well. J. H. Yoder discusses Luke well in his *The Politics of Jesus* (Grand Rapids, Mich.: Eerdmans, 1972), chaps. 2, 3.

[11]That tradition assumes that "the poor" are pious, for dependence on God is the characteristic of the poor (to whom else can they turn?) and that they are oppressed, for we have yet to find an author who uses the title "the poor" without indicating at least his perception of some actual suffering. In late Judaism that title designated the pious sufferer (e.g., the *Psalms of Solomon,* where it refers to the Maccabean *Hasidim*) or the elect of God (as opposed to the rich in 1 Enoch 108). In the War Scroll from Qumran (1QM) it refers to the oppressed group which receives the eschatological victory. That scroll actually uses the term "poor in spirit" ('anwê rûaḥ, 1QM XIV, 7) to designate those to whom God is promising victory over their rich oppressors.

[12]That meaning of "merciful" is clear in Greek when we compare the "merciful" *('eleēmones)* who receive mercy *('eleēthēsontai)* of Matthew 5:7 with those giving alms *('eleēmosunē)* in 6:2ff. Charity was very much a part of mercy in Jewish thought.

[13]The reason for believing that the summaries are paradigmatic in Acts is the following: Early in Acts Luke discusses the Jerusalem church structure fairly fully, which gives the reader a picture of what a church is, but then Luke never raises the topic again. He handles his sermons similarly, for he abbreviates in later sermons material recorded in greater detail in earlier sermons. The Jerusalem practice also explains some of the material in 2 Thessalonians. See note 20. On the problem of the descriptive and normative, see G. Fee, "Hermeneutics and Historical Precedent" in R. P. Spittler, ed., *Perspectives on the New Pentecostalism* (Grand Rapids, Mich.: Baker, 1976), pp. 119-132.

[14]E. Haenchen, *The Acts of the Apostles* (Oxford: Basil Blackwell, 1971), p. 192, and F. F. Bruce, *The Book of Acts* (Grand Rapids, Mich.: Eerdmans, 1954), p. 108. K. Lake, in *The Beginnings of Christianity* ([London: Macmillan, 1933], vol. V, p. 140), comments, "The expenses of life were covered by the periodic sale of property, and by the use of all possessions to help the needy."

[15]Luke certainly believes that the church is fulfilling the promise of Deuteronomy 15:4-5 and possibly that it is fulfilling the goal of hellenistic fellowships. Yoder and R. B. Sloan, *The Favorable Year of the Lord* (Austin: Univ. of Texas Press, 1977), both argue that in his summaries in Acts Luke reinterprets the Jubilee year of Leviticus 25 (which has also been programmatic for the preaching of Jesus) in terms of the new, non-agricultural Christian community: Jubilee is fulfilled when the rich share their goods with the poor. We find this exegesis attractive, but have yet to be totally convinced by it.

[16]I am assuming an exegesis of James in this paragraph which I have worked out more fully in *Themes in the Epistle of James that are Judaistic in Character* (unpublished U. Manchester thesis, 1974) and in "Tradition and Citation in the Epistle of James" in W. W. Gasque and W. S. LaSor, ed., *Scripture, Tradition and Interpretation* (Grand Rapids, Mich.: Eerdmans, 1978). I hope to establish it in more accessible form in a commentary which is now in progress.

[17]I have ignored the motive of pleasing others, since it is subordinate to the other two themes and found mostly in 1 Corinthians. For an interesting discussion of the interplay of law and Spirit in Paul, showing why 1 Corinthians in particular is full of rules drawn from the surrounding cultural mores, see J. Drane, *Paul, Libertine or Legalist?* (London: SPCK,

1975). R. Schnackenburg's *The Moral Teaching of the New Testament* (New York: Seabury, 1965) is also important for this entire discussion, as is V. P. Furnish's *Theology and Ethics in Paul* (Nashville: Abingdon Press, 1968) for the Pauline discussion.

[18]Eph. 5:21; cf. 1 Pet. 2:11—3:12; Phil. 2:1-4; Gal. 6:1ff.; Rom. 13:1ff. Notice that in those passages Paul comes closest to Stoic ethics. Subordination is not something which the other party is to demand of one, but is voluntary, Spirit-directed from within one. Subordination is also not exactly symmetrical (whether of government-citizens, parents-children, or of husband-wife); Paul has the ability to combine hierarchy and equality in a fashion foreign to the modern mind.

[19]Generosity would be the corresponding virtue. For details and passages see L. H. Marshall, *The Challenge of New Testament Ethics* (London: Macmillan, 1966), pp. 286-288.

[20]1 Thess. 3:6-13 speaks of those who are sponging off the generosity of the community, which indicates that Paul had established some system of sharing with poorer members of the community. Paul does not dismantle the system when abuses crop up, but instead demands that the sluggards work and contribute to the common fund (or else suffer excommunication). He encourages the other Christians to continue sharing. Let us "not be weary in well-doing" (Gal. 6:9). A similar problem is regulated in the *Didache* 11-13.

[21]Although the Jerusalem community held a special place for Paul, partly since his fellowship with it would insure the unity of the Jewish and gentile missions, the principles he discusses in no way refer to Jerusalem as a special case, only to their poverty. Some have suggested that Jerusalem needed support because they had unwisely engaged in their "communal experiment" in the first flush of their conversion. But that ignores several factors: (1) As the center of Christianity Jerusalem was responsible for the support of many apostles, prophets, etc., who resided there for shorter or longer periods of time. (2) Since many Jews returned to Jerusalem to die, it is likely that the church had a high proportion of older converts. (3) It is likely that much of the early persecution took the form of economic discrimination. (4) Jerusalem's natural economic situation was poor at best and suffered several reverses during the apostolic period, as J. Jeremias shows in *Jerusalem in the Times of Jesus* (London: SCM Press, 1969), pp. 120ff.

[22]Reference might also be made to apocalyptic literature, specifically to the book of Revelation. There it is harder to view the lifestyle of the church on earth, the one possible hint being that the first love of Ephesus may refer to love for one another expressed in sharing more than to

love for God. Revelation is full of the characteristic distrust of wealth and the world, however. The dominant image of the end is Babylon, the anti-God prostitute cited not only for her political intrigues but also for her commercial dominance. She enriches the merchants of the earth, so her destruction means ruin for all the wealthy and powerful. The call to the Christian in that context is, "Come out of her" (Rev. 18). The prophet argues that the Christian lifestyle is not to be that of the world, for to be caught in its methods and goals would be to risk sharing the judgment of God. Cf. J. Ellul, *Apocalypse* (New York, 1977).

[23]Slavery is a case in point, for Paul's teaching on the brotherhood of believers was so destructive of it within the church that in the early fathers one finds that it was common upon conversion to free one's slaves. But neither Paul nor anyone else in the first few hundred years of the church suggested that slavery as an institution outside of the church needed attacking. Of course Paul was not living in a governmental system which claimed to represent him.

[24]Rom. 13:11-14; 1 Cor. 5:9-13; 6:9-11; Eph. 4:19.

[25]Mt. 6:16-18; Mk. 2:18-22; 1 Cor. 7:5.

STRUGGLING FREE IN THE FAMILY: GUIDELINES AND MODELS

4.

Chapters four through six are perhaps the most important in this book. Careful thinking about biblical foundations and about how the urgent need for evangelism and social justice summon us to a simpler lifestyle are important. But a few living examples are frequently worth many chapters of theory—hence the three chapters of concrete models of a simpler lifestyle for families, churches and professional people.

The first two sections of chapter four provide some general guidelines by Elaine M. Amerson and the Mennonite Central Committee for moving toward a simpler lifestyle in the family. Then eight people tell the stories of their own pilgrimages toward simplicity.

No one claims to have arrived. No one offers their story in

a legalistic, self-righteous way as a norm for all Christian families. Rather, they share their stories here—as they did in the panel discussion at the Consultation—in the hope that their personal pilgrimage may assist others on the slow but joyful journey.

CHRISTIAN FAMILY LIFESTYLE GUIDELINES:
Elaine M. Amerson

About thirty miles from Lexington, Kentucky, is a restored Shaker village. That nineteenth-century religious group was committed to living in "creative simplicity." I spent eight years of my life just half an hour's drive from that town with its rich religious history, but it was not until ten years later that I began to appreciate that history. When I lived nearby I was more interested in the buildings' separate entrances for men and women. I overlooked the emphasis on a biblical call to live responsibly and faithfully as stewards of the earth. It's tragic that I missed that salient point since my own Wesleyan heritage had similar calls to simplicity. In 1973 a group met in Shakertown and drew up a document that captured the spirit of the Shaker heritage. It is known as the Shakertown Pledge:[1]

> *Recognizing that the earth and the fulness thereof is a gift from our gracious God, and that we are called to cherish, nurture, and provide loving stewardship for the earth's resources,*
>
> *And recognizing that life itself is a gift, and a call to responsibility, joy, and celebration, I make the following declarations:*
>
> *1. I declare myself to be a world citizen.*
> *2. I commit myself to lead an ecologically sound life.*
> *3. I commit myself to lead a life of creative simplicity and to share my personal wealth with the world's poor.*
> *4. I commit myself to join with others in reshaping institutions in order to bring about a more just global society*

in which each person has full access to the needed resources for their physical, emotional, intellectual, and spiritual growth.

5. I commit myself to occupational accountability, and in so doing I will seek to avoid the creation of products which cause harm to others.

6. I affirm the gift of my body, and commit myself to its proper nourishment and physical well-being.

7. I commit myself to examine continually my relations with others, and to attempt to relate honestly, morally, and lovingly to those around me.

8. I commit myself to personal renewal through prayer, meditation, and study.

9. I commit myself to responsible participation in a community of faith.

The spirit of that pledge calls for good stewardship, for responsible and joyful living. All of those things I can affirm. I would, however, like to call for the affirmation of such posture from a "We" stance instead of the individualistic "I" who makes a singular commitment. Along with the "I declare" and "I commit" there should be some corporate declarations and commitments. In other words, it seems that our position should be one of covenanting together, as members of the body of Christ, to pursue such bold commitments. We need to be making those statements as groups of faithful Christians, turning the "I's" into "We's." One such "We" grouping is the family.

The thesis I would propose is that Christian families are called to lifestyles marked by biblical simplicity and that on the horizon substantial change is occurring in our society's lifestyle perceptions. It therefore may be incumbent on Christian families to chart the course for lifestyles which are both simple and just. We are called to find a new course amid the treacherous waters of poorly distributed global resources. I would further suggest some guidelines and resources for families in preliminary consideration of this journey.

The biblical call. It is first necessary to affirm the biblical, theological call to simplicity. John V. Taylor in *Enough is Enough* masterfully sets forth the "theology of enough." He speaks of the dream of "shalom" as something broader than "peace"; it is "the harmony of a caring community informed *at every point* by its awareness of God. . . . It meant a dancing kind of inter-relationship, seeking something more free than equality, more generous than equity, the ever-shifting equipoise of a life system."[2] There are crucial images to be gleaned from the Scriptures, both the Old and New Testaments: admonishings against greed and covetousness (lust and domination); the law of Jubilee (and its principle that one does not own the land in perpetuity); manna in the wilderness (which could not be hoarded); the law of gleaning (not reaping to the edges of the fields); the call for justice —caring for the poor, hungry, needy, oppressed; giving of the firstfruits—tithing; sharing from abundance with those in need (as the church in Acts); admonitions against usury —charging exorbitant interest.

Those images take biblical shape in the context of a covenanted family. The facets of the picture include husbands and wives, parents and children, sisters and brothers, intergenerational relations—all of whom interact in nurturing and honoring, naming and valuing, managing and caring, dreaming and creating a Now and a Future. And because there is an understanding of the breaking of the kingdom of God into the present, there is room for the calling together of isolated persons into family relationships of faith. People who hear the words of hope and obedience—discipleship is not solitary—can move into the arena of promise only as they share in appropriate relationships: "But you are a chosen race, a royal priesthood, a holy nation, God's own people, that you may declare the wonderful deeds of him who called you out of darkness into his marvelous light. Once you were no people but now you are God's people; once you had not received mercy but now you have received mercy" (1 Pet. 2:9-10).

Thus the biblical view of family included the traditional view of an extended blood family and our current norm of the nuclear family, as well as a radical idea of covenantal bodies of faithful and committed persons coming together under the lordship of Christ. Those understandings grew out of a culture where family patterns reflected and supported strong family ties in a context of strong covenantal community ties. It is, for example, important to note that most of the early churches—like that of Mary, John Mark's mother (Acts 12:12)—were in houses. I like to think of these as home churches or household churches or, in today's language, as extended-family-and-friend churches.

The floundering family. Today the family is in transition. When we hear "family," most of us probably think of Mom and Dad and the kids, the nuclear family. That is a relatively modern outlook, however; the concept and structure of nuclear families have emerged since World War 2. With their arrival came seeds of isolation and alienation. The nuclear family is in trouble. Only one family in eight today is that typical North American family portrayed in the Dick and Jane readers, the "ideal" where there are "two parents, children, Dad going to work, Mom staying home." Ozzie and Harriet are no longer the norm, if they ever were.

Today Mom and Dad live together less and less. In 1976, twenty percent of the children under age eighteen lived with only one parent. The trend appears to be increasing as the divorce rate rises. Amitai Etzioni suggests that "if the present rate of increase in divorce and single households continues to accelerate as it did for the last ten years, by mid-1990 not one American family will be left."[3]

Working parents are the rule now instead of the exception.

Since 1975 the majority of children in this country have lived in a home where both parents or the only parent, worked during the day. I am strongly supportive of the new freedom being exercised by women in the marketplace. We should be employed. The problem is not with working women, but with family and parent styles which no longer fit the circumstances.

Abuse and violence, which cut across race, class and background, are increasing in the home. Approximately one-fourth of all murders in the U.S. occur within the family. And perhaps more tragic is the fact that at least ten percent of the children who witness parental violence eventually become batterers as adults.

In our society, which has seen the dispersion of the extended family, the nuclear family is isolated and may be coming unglued. We are looking for new directions. One new concept is that of the multiadult family or the intentional extended family. That model is seen in such divergent activities as Big Brothers/Sisters on the one hand and as many adults living together on the other. Another model is community living, which may mean separate households living in proximity and relating closely, as opposed to multiadult common-household living. The hunger for new structures of intimacy is reflected in the interaction of small "groups of meaning" which have been called *ersatz* or functional religions, or in emerging family substitutes (like Parents Without Partners or Weight Watchers).

In addition to changes in family groupings, an emerging concern with lifestyle is signaled in the new emphasis on voluntary simplicity. A perceptible change is occurring in regard to lifestyle today. In the spring of 1977 a Harris poll discovered that seventy-nine percent of North Americans would emphasize "teaching people how to live more with basic essentials" and that only seventeen percent would support "reaching higher standards of living." That poll found that sixty-six percent endorsed the "breaking up of big things and getting back to more humanized living" over "developing bigger and more efficient ways of doing things," and that sixty-three percent believed in putting greater emphasis on learning to appreciate human values instead of material values. E. F. Schumacher in *Small is Beautiful* captures the sentiment of the trend away from *Big* and *More*. Today more people talk of choosing a simple lifestyle, of voluntary poverty, and of emphasizing intangibles over consumptive patterns that use up nonrenewable resources.

Even the business community has caught on: "In 1975, Arnold Mitchell and Duane Elgin published for the Stanford Research Institute what has turned out to be the most popular Business Intelligence report in the history of the institute on "Voluntary Simplicity." The report predicts that the "fastest growing consumer market of the coming decades" may well be among those who live by the tenet of a simpler lifestyle. . . . the projection in this report [is] that the number of persons espousing a simpler lifestyle may climb from five million in 1977 to over sixty million people with a spending power of $300 billion dollars by the year 2000."[4]

Biblical alternatives. The call for us as Christians amid such flux is to discern and appropriate biblical values for families in the 1980s. The beginning point is to affirm the nature of the family as the context for community—it stands against individualism but for the person.

Key factors vital to a nurturing family are identified by Virginia Satir as: high *self-worth*; direct, clear, specific, honest *communication*; flexible, human, appropriate *rules* which are subject to change; and an open and hopeful *link to society*.[5] The family must be interactive within its bounds and with other persons and groups in the "outside" world.

So, while we live in a consumption-oriented, success-driven society, we must return to values that have been a part of our evangelical Christian heritage. The following values seem imperative to the Christian family today:

Justice	as opposed to	—Oppression
Sharing	as opposed to	—Selfishness
Quality (not quantity)	as opposed to	—Gluttony (buying more)
Responsible use of resources	as opposed to	—Using up resources
Peacemaking	as opposed to	—Violence/Dominance
Joyful living	as opposed to	—Drudgery
Health (exercise and good foods)	as opposed to	—Sickness
Community (being together)	as opposed to	—Individualism/Loneliness
Obedience	as opposed to	—Aimlessness
Grace	as opposed to	—Guilt
Covenant/Trust	as opposed to	—Contracts/Punishment

To choose a simpler family lifestyle based on these values is an act of faith. It is a means of sharing and a celebration of our freedom. It is rich in a creativity and spirituality that allow us to direct our energies toward persons and away from things. In my family we approach simplicity by employing several tenets set forth in *Enough is Enough:*

1. Join the joyful resistance movement by claiming, "The price tag is too high."

2. Refuse to be conned by asking, "Who are you kidding?" That question works particularly well for commercials on television. Even our three-year-old understands the power in it.

3. Travel light by repeating, "You can't take it with you!" That leads to an attitude of sharing resources.

4. Be a family for defiance by finding ways of living in a corporate opposition that shouts out, "Things don't have to be like this."

Many suggestions for families living more simply are now being made. I offer the following as guidelines for a family beginning to be aware of a need to simplify its lifestyle:

1. Start prayerfully with the Scriptures, understanding that God gives specific direction about those who are poor and how those with abundance should relate.

2. Become familiar with the facts of overconsumption and individualization in our society.

3. Begin as a family to discuss and understand your resources and the responsibility that accompanies them.

4. Find out about poverty in your local area and get in touch with persons who are poor.

5. Expand your understanding of poverty to a global awareness of the interrelatedness of all of life.

6. Plan strategies as a family and then take a first step toward simplification. Then take another—and another. Don't expect change to occur overnight; patterns weren't established quickly and won't be broken instantly either.

7. Emphasize the joyful life. Don't go on a "guilt trip." Look for ways to make the journey fun.

8. Talk with others who are attempting to simplify their lifestyles. Read books and magazines that will keep you in touch with such persons and ideas.

9. Become creative with interaction times, both as a family and with other families, persons and groups.

10. Celebrate your successes.

Further help for families trying to live simply will be found in the following sections of chapter four. In particular, the Mennonite Central Committee's publication "Spare and Share," which is reprinted here, will serve as a valuable tool for individuals and families.

The family is one of those God-sanctioned building blocks which we may employ to structure our world. Just as surely as chromosomes carry the genetic traits of human beings, families are the carriers of lifestyles and the typical arena for lifestyle choices. There are strong biblical models of how families contribute to people's values. While we acknowledge the fragility of the family in our impersonal, institutional-industrial society, we can point with confidence to the biblical foundations that undergird and strengthen the family. At Walter Brueggemann has suggested, "The faith-family thus is an opening for a new history in which all of life may be a zone of freedom and security. That is the family promised in the Gospel."[6] For "simplicity" to become more than a catchword for Honda or Grape-Nuts commercials, it will take the family to bring realistic choices for simplicity into the daily lives of us all.

As a microcosm of the interactive agents found in all of life, the family survives. We continue to "muddle through" gloriously!

SPARE AND SHARE: Mennonite Central Committee[7]

Spare and Share is a starter action list for people concerned about world hunger. The following suggestions are for conserving food and energy and challenging policies that oppress the hungry.

Although there is no instant pipeline for sharing with hungry people what we spare, there are valid reasons for creatively reducing our consumption. Most important are the repeated themes in the Bible of sharing with the poor and hungry, taking responsibility for each other and finding contentment with basic necessities of life rather than striving after wealth (Is. 58:1-12; Mt. 6:25-34; 1 Tim. 6:6-10). God's judgment is on the covetousness, greed and insensitivity of the rich (Amos 4—6; Lk. 6:24-25).

This basic Christian motivation speaks not only to what we do, but to what kind of people we are. Living simply will give us more credibility as we work to help the poor. Changes we advocate for others must grow from our own experience. One Mennonite church leader said, "We cannot be great overseas if we're not great at home."

The amount of food and energy wasted daily in North America is staggering. But perhaps more serious than the actual volume wasted is the attitude caught and transmitted to the next generation—that food and energy are "easy-come, easy-go" commodities. Such an attitude will poorly serve our children as they grow up in a world of scarcity.

One of the best ways today to translate savings to action is to give funds saved to church agencies for hunger programs. There are many ways for congregations to encourage and dramatize such commitments.

Use this list as a beginning point. Putting a few ideas into practice will revise and expand your understanding of how to spare and share.

Give as Freely as You Receive

1. Place ten percent of food-budget money in a designated receptacle as part of Sunday worship experience. Send the money to service and relief agencies.

2. Establish scholarship funds for persons interested in agriculture, nutrition or community development in needy areas of the world. Encourage people to train for those vocations.

3. Participate in local CROP (Christian Rural Overseas Program) fund-raising activities such as walkathons.

4. Plan with family and friends to give money to hunger programs as an alternative to exchanging Christmas gifts.

Life Is More than Food

5. Fast one day a week or skip the equivalent meals.

6. Reduce intake of animal proteins. Most Americans eat twice their Recommended Daily Allowance of protein. Learn how to get more of the protein requirement from plant sources.

7. Reduce intake of sugar and coffee to protect your health, to save money and to encourage Third-World countries to use agricultural land for more nutritious food crops.

8. Eliminate highly processed and overpackaged foods from your diet and redevelop a taste for grains (bread and cereals), beans and soybeans, vegetables and fruits.

9. Grow a garden as a family/fellowship project and freeze or can the produce.

10. Buy food directly from those who raise it, if possible.

11. Compost fruit and vegetable peelings and other food residues to enrich the soil near your home.

12. Avoid using commercial fertilizers on lawns or other nonfood-producing areas.

13. Use part of your own lawn for gardening. Develop community gardens on institutional land. Encourage gardening on school land as educational projects.

14. Ask local public schools to work at the problem of waste in their cafeterias. Challenge administrators not only with the quantity of food wasted, but with values children absorb when they participate in food waste. Visit or write state and national officials (school administrators can tell you whom to contact) and urge them to work at this concern.

15. Work toward removing vending machines with non-nutritious food from schools, institutions and businesses. Encourage vending machines or snack bars with more nutritious, low-cost food.

16. Avoid fast-food restaurants where waste of precooked foods and disposable containers is usually heavy, and food is of dubious nutritional value.

17. If possible, carry lunches when you know you must eat away from home.

Purses that Don't Grow Old

18. Walk, bike or use public transportation whenever possible. Carpool when you can. Support public transportation development.

19. Use small cars.

20. Keep track of how much heating fuel, water and electricity your household uses each month (quantities are listed on utility bills). Work at reducing the figures whenever possible. Do the same in businesses and institutions if you are in a position to do so.

21. Plan recreation that gives physical exercise and/or builds relationships but uses little fuel or other nonrenewable resources. Consider biking, hiking, gardening,

walking, playing games, visiting, singing, painting, hobbies and crafts.

22. Find lodging with friends when you're away from home and invite people to use your home. Motels, besides being expensive, tend to put agricultural land on the edge of cities out of production and use vast amounts of resources to build, heat, cool and otherwise maintain. Camp for the same reasons if you can do it without large investment in equipment.

23. In farming, work at developing production methods that use less energy.

24. Recycle glass, aluminum and paper, but equally important, use less of those commodities. Ask your community garbage service to provide a recycling system even if it means raising the cost.

25. Use fewer disposables. Examples: carry your own cup instead of using styrofoam throwaways; use cloth diapers except for travel; wipe up spills with rags or sponges. Challenge the trend toward more and more disposables in hospitals and other institutions.

Godliness with Contentment

26. Determine to be free from clothing fashions and fads. Learn to live with a smaller, more basic wardrobe. Buy or sew good quality clothing in basic styles and wear garments until they wear out.

27. Mend and reactivate old clothing instead of buying new.

28. Buy used furniture and appliances and reactivate them. Learn to live with fewer appliances and less furniture. Reject fads in home decoration and rely on your own ingenuity.

29. Move into a smaller house or share a large house with more people.

30. Instead of houseware, jewelry or other selling parties, entertain your friends at quiltings, canning bees, mending

parties, bread-making demonstrations, soap-makings.

__31.__ Stop shopping for recreation. Shopping malls have become our new community centers, built on the foundation of consumerism and affluence. Shop only when you have a list of things that the household really needs. Find more satisfying forms of recreation, other reasons to get out of the house.

32. Buy at small business places where you can develop personal relationships and make your concerns felt. Large chain stores are usually controlled by larger corporations which push growth, more stores, more blacktop, more heating, cooling and lighting, more land and energy u~ed for consumer enterprises. Small savings one may make in such places are not worth the gas used driving to them and the resources wasted in maintaining them at a growth level.

Swords into Plowshares

33. Work to protect agricultural land in your community from being developed for other purposes. Government officials at local and federal levels should be encouraged to support land-use legislation safeguarding productive agricultural acreage from housing and business developments.

34. Members of government should be undergirded in efforts to reduce military spending and arms sales to other countries. Urge government to convert weapons research and arms production into agricultural research programs to benefit Third-World food production.

35. Study the role of "agribusiness" as carried out by corporations both in North America and in underdeveloped countries. Where multinational (agribusiness) corporations have served to widen the disparity between rich and poor and to eliminate small farmers, they must be curbed.

36. Support government food policies committed to world food security (adequate food aid and a national grain bank) and rural development for small farmers in food-deficit countries.

The Household of God

37. Hunger is still widespread in North America, though it may be hidden from our view. Malnutrition among the elderly, minority groups and the unemployed is particularly common. Find out if there are hungry people living within ten miles of your church. Study the problem and the work of existing agencies. Determine what your church can do to help.

38. See if your church building can be used during the week in a program of mission to the community.

39. Meet as a congregation or in small groups to discuss this list and add to it. Can you agree on any specific changes people will make and then pledge your support for each other?

These thirty-nine items represent the accumulated wisdom of the Mennonite Central Committee. The contributions which follow are the stories of individuals and families who have begun to search for ways of simplifying their lifestyles.

A JOURNEY TOWARD SIMPLICITY: Walter and Virginia Hearn

[Walter and Virginia Hearn were unable to attend the Consultation in New Jersey, but they contributed to the dialog by sending each participant a printed statement of their thoughts.[8]]

A few years ago we sensed that God wanted us to do something different with our lives, but we didn't realize how radical a change it would be.

The competitive professional rat race left us little time to think and write. We had seen what happens to families when a husband spends himself and all his time at a demanding job. Even with two children to support and Ginny's elderly mother to care for, we felt there must be another way for us.

We were willing to trust God and "count the cost" of trying something different, some way of working together in a new kind of life. So we kept careful records and deliberately pared our cost of living down to half our income. By saving the other half, each year on the payroll "bought" us a year to experiment. We stayed two years, then took the plunge and moved to Berkeley.

Our family enterprise (writing and editing) doesn't support us yet, but we seldom panic. God has been teaching us how much we can do without. He has reinforced our basic decision in various ways, and provided bits of income to keep us in "bread" and hope. We think he intends for us to survive. So now we have made another decision: Whenever we do begin to earn more money, we are resolved not to let our "standard of living" rise along with our income. We are beginning to feel liberated.

Cutting down: 1973. Cutting down doesn't come easy in our society. Possessions have become the measure of everything, even of spiritual worth, and commercial interests control or dominate most channels of communication. What we have done goes against the American grain.

We think that deliberately lowering our standard of living in obedience to God is part of what Jesus meant by being "poor in spirit." The amazing thing is that the quality of our life seems higher than before.

Of course, we have to beware of the reverse snobbery of spiritual one-up-manship. No matter how little one learns to live on, even that comes at the expense of someone else. What each of us has is a gift, no matter how we stand financially. Greed tempts the poor as well as the rich. Christians need not put down people who are wealthy, wasteful, extravagant or stingy, as long as we don't follow their ways. God is their judge, and ours. We ought rather to put our energy into being examples of a better way, just as Jesus Christ is ours. Each person must live his or her own life as

God leads them. We don't want to overgeneralize from our experience. Our Father seems to love variety.

In a sense, we have become more "materialistic." That is, we care more about the way we use the "materials" of our life. We want to "have dominion over created things," rather than abusing them or letting them control us. Here are some practical steps we've already taken.

We stay out of stores as much as possible. We go to Salvation Army outlets for most of our clothes, to day-old bakery shops, to supermarkets for sale items, occasionally to flea markets. But we shop prudently at them all. Secondhand bargains may come from classified ads, co-op bulletin boards or garage sales. For books we first try libraries, then secondhand bookstores. A cheap wok and some chopsticks keep us out of Chinese restaurants except for "occasions," and then we go for lunch, not expensive dinners.

Our home menu features many "clean-out-the-icebox" soups, each as unique as you will find in a quaint foreign restaurant. Bones for our soup stock are more often cheap chicken backs than beef or pork. And the compost pile gets whatever doesn't go into the soup pot, because someday we want our backyard to be a productive vegetable garden. Gardening is one of the trades we have yet to learn.

Taking care of the possessions we have has more appeal than buying new ones. "Making do" is the educational side of doing without. Clothes, shoes, appliances, tools—almost anything can be kept in use with glue, patches, tape, baling wire and ingenuity. The fifty-year-old, run-down house we're buying is an education in itself. But the more of ourselves we put into it, the more it becomes ours—ours and the Lord's.

We've become alert scavengers in vacant lots and junk piles, delighting to find some use for what other people discard. Our waffle iron was someone's throwaway, but it works. Foraging has supplied berries, nuts, fruit and fireplace wood that otherwise would have gone to waste.

Driving a VW makes scrounging easier and shopping cheaper, but we try not to "run around." Instead we plan trips to include several errands in one vicinity. We walk as much as we can for economy, health and ecology, and often take a bus instead of driving our car.

Since "entertainment" is such an expensive luxury, it is worth scanning the newspaper for low-cost movies, plays and musical events. And there are museums and parks to explore. Simple pleasures, like reading, walking, talking with friends, playing tennis, inviting people home for a meal, are more rewarding than most activities for which you have to pay. Coming from the flatlands, it's a great treat for us just to be up high enough to look out over the city, day or night. The view reminds us to thank God for bringing us here, to this particular and beautiful place. And the price is right.

Thoughts on voluntary poverty. The price was also right (free) when we taught a course in "simple living" for the Crucible (a Christian "free university" then in existence in our city). We called our course "Blessed Are the Poor," and with another couple shared what we've all learned about living poor—"in spirit" and "with spirit." Brothers and sisters in Christ exchanged specifics on low-cost living in this area and came home with new ideas to try. The course gave us a chance to think about theory as well as practice. We came up with ten arguments for "living poor" as a radical Christian way of life:

1. Voluntary poverty identifies us with the poor; that is, with most of the people in God's world. What sense does it make for Christians to say we're here to serve people, if we haven't tried to learn from experience something about how most of the world lives?

2. Voluntary poverty may be the only way to sustain religious revival. The Bible warns of the danger of riches. John Wesley preached the gospel to grubby have-nots in England,

saw them become joyful Christians, sober up, prosper, then fall away. Wesley sorrowfully concluded: "Wherever riches have increased, the essence of religion has decreased in the same proportion. Therefore, I do not see how it is possible, in the nature of things, for any revival of religion to continue long. For religion must necessarily produce both industry and frugality, and these cannot but produce riches. But as riches increase, so will pride, anger, and love of the world in all its branches."[9]

3. Voluntary poverty is an ecological imperative. The world simply can't afford the kind of consumer mentality spawned in the U.S. and rapidly being copied elsewhere. Is a daily newspaper a necessity or a luxury? If every person in the world insisted on having one, how long would the world's forests last? Are Christians to be stewards or squanderers of what God has put on the earth? In his superb piece entitled "Think Little," Wendell Berry says that a lot of the counterculture is still pervaded by the consumer mentality, the desire to be "in."[10] Are we willing to be "out of it"? Will we do what is right, even if we find ourselves alone in doing it? If Christians aren't willing to "think little," who is?

4. Voluntary poverty is an effective political tool in the American marketplace economy. Want to be a Christian revolutionary? The revolution that can really change this country is the personal, spiritual revolution that gives people the guts to shun seductive advertising and status symbols. In the U.S., money talks. And it talks just as loud when we don't spend it as when we do. The military-industrial complex may foster the throwaway mentality for its own ends, but when we stop buying, it stops making a profit. Joel Fort, a San Francisco Bay area psychiatrist, gave up a big income to involve himself more deeply in society's needs. Interviewed in a magazine for middle-aged dropouts, he called what he was doing "the brick-by-brick rebuilding of society."[11] Changing yourself and those around you, Fort said, will

eventually change society, "but it will never be changed by mayors, governors, and presidents, particularly by the low-caliber, hypocritical mediocrities that we now have in elective office in America, and who are nominated by both parties in our society."

5. Voluntary poverty makes possible alternative (low-paid) vocations of social significance. The bimonthly formerly called *Vocations for Social Change*, published in Canyon, California, is now called *Workforce*. Since 1969 it has been calling "young America" to radical alternatives. The VSC Collective is radical politically, but many spiritually radical Christians would make the same point: If as a single person it costs you, say, $6,000 a year to live, you're locked into the wasteful, spiritually destructive "American way of life." Cut your expenses to half of that, and you can afford to take a lower-paying job that makes a difference in the world.

6. Voluntary poverty strengthens the pacifist position by providing a "moral equivalent of war." On the eve of World War 1, William James (the psychologist and pacifist) gave a powerful lecture called "The Moral Equivalent of War."[12] War will never be easy to stamp out, he argued, because love of "the strong life" is bred into us. After all, we are descended from the *winners* of all those bloody battles of history. Pacifism sounds like a sissy alternative to hardy military life. We need some "moral equivalent" that can call up our courage, determination, self-sacrifice and spirit of brotherhood the way war always has. What could do that better than altruistic, voluntary poverty? Living at subsistence level and sharing our surplus with others is no sissy life. It is an all-out "spiritual warfare" against pride, lust, greed and the horror they ultimately breed: war.

7. Voluntary poverty provides a kind of security and freedom unobtainable in any other way. Most people see the point about freedom, especially if they've read Thoreau's marvelous chapter on "Economy" in *Walden*.[13] But people

hold onto expensive lifestyles because of their high-paying jobs, kidding themselves that they are trading freedom for security. What happens when economic changes wipe out those industries or those jobs, as has happened to thousands of heavily mortgaged Ph.D.'s? Where is security when savings are eroded by inflation? Poverty of spirit builds the only real security: practice at trusting God; skill at coping with change; the interdependence of sharing; knowledge that hard times can be survived. "How vigilant we are!" cried Thoreau. "Determined not to live by faith if we can avoid it!"

8. Voluntary poverty builds constructive human relationships by making us dependent on each other. "Doing without" makes us appreciate public transportation, parks, libraries, co-ops, families. Private ownership, in spite of its obvious advantages, is an alienating influence in American society. In *Journal of a Walden Two Commune*, the participants say their reason for holding property in common is that "it saves money and makes sense."[14] But when people live together or use the same tool or share anything, they have to learn to work together or their hassles will destroy them, as those Twin Oaks communards found out.

Christians can get new ideas from many sources and build on the experience of others. The magazine *The Mother Earth News* is one place to learn how to survive on little. "Living poor" teaches us to pick up workable ideas wherever we can and to share them with brothers and sisters. It's a life based on sharing, in fact, whether we live in a commune, in a family or alone.

9. Voluntary poverty tends to make life more educational and education more relevant to life. Joan Ranson Shortney, in *How to Live on Nothing*, says, "The secret of living joyfully on nothing is in taking a little time to do things that the majority of people pay to have done."[15] And how educational that can be. Ernest Callenbach, in *Living Poor With Style*, says, "Our education is hopelessly impractical in equipping

us to cope with our own necessities. In order to defend your
biological dignity in such a situation, it is important to gain
confidence in your own ability to produce and repair everything that is genuinely essential to survival. The list of such
things is not as long as you might imagine."[16]

10. Finally, voluntary poverty reminds us of the spiritual
significance of everything we do. Everything we have, not
just a tithe, belongs to God. Everything we are has come from
God—house, books, education, income, health, life, time. To
be poor in spirit is to use all these things joyfully, responsibly, unselfishly, gratefully. It is, in fact, to live abundantly.

Jesus tells us not to fret. Our Father feeds the birds of the
air and clothes the lilies of the field—and what's more, he
does it with style. "But if God so clothes the grass of the field,
which today is alive and tomorrow is thrown into the oven,
will he not much more clothe you, O men of little faith?
Therefore do not be anxious, saying, 'What shall we eat?' or
'What shall we drink?' or 'What shall we wear?' For the Gen-
tiles seek all these things; and your heavenly Father knows
that you need them all. But seek first his kingdom and his
righteousness, and all these things shall be yours as well"
(Mt. 6:30-33).

Walt's thoughts on recycling: 1974. I think our family would
recycle things for fun even if it didn't make so much sense.
But part of the fun is knowing that it makes sense.

This article was written on the backs of questionnaires
from some professor's research project. He (or somebody
cleaning out his office) dumped a big box of papers and IBM
cards in a vacant lot. We did our Berkeley environment a
favor by picking up his litter. And we got a favor in return:
free typing paper.

Paper is made from trees, and we don't like to see trees (or
anything else) wasted. "The earth is the Lord's" says Psalm
24, "and everything in it" (NIV). We think we ought to take
good care of it.

When that psalm was written, materials were plentiful and people were scarce. Now it's the other way around and getting worse. If the present American way of life continues the earth's resources will eventually be stripped and the population will be buried in garbage.

The day we found the "waste paper," we also picked up some driftwood. I built shelves out of it with salvaged nails straightened with a hammer. For paint I used the dregs in a discarded paint can. The can itself was cruddy with caked paint, so I put it under the workbench to catch dangerous, dirty or absolutely unusable trash.

Tin cans, bottles and newspapers that we cannot reuse ourselves, we take to a recycling center. We save all kinds of containers, as long as we have room, for possible future use: hardware, pieces of wood, metal, plastic, leather, cloth and so on. Surplus household items (furniture, books, tools, clothing) that are immediately usable are given to people who need them. Anything combustible, like wood chips or yard prunings, ends up as fireplace kindling. Grass cuttings and most kitchen waste go back into the soil as compost.

We can never think of a use for everything, of course, and we accumulate more of some things than one family can use. (Anybody need a few thousand punched IBM cards? A dozen clean cider jugs?) Recycling does for the imagination what jogging does for the circulation.

When our kids were small, they were the envy of our Iowa neighborhood. For their expensive toys? No, for a backyard "fort" of fallen elm logs with a sewer-pipe "cannon" mounted on old lawnmower wheels. And for some huge scrounged crates that turned our basement into a castle and then a pirate ship and then whatever they wanted it to be. Teaching children to transform old things instead of having to buy new ones is a rich gift to give to them—and to the world.

For his fourteenth birthday, our son, Russ, invited a friend out for pizza. Then we took the two of them to the edge of the city dump. "Since it's your birthday," said the Last of the Big-Time Spenders, "you can have anything you find. Good hunting!" Hours later, Russ came back with a phonograph turntable in perfect condition. His friend thought it was the most fabulous "birthday party" he'd ever been to.

Foraging or "gathering manna" is great adventure, but you don't have to go that far. Just stay alert and receive with thanksgiving whatever God provides. From friends we helped move, we inherited an old vacuum cleaner with a defective switch. I learned a few things trying to repair it. The switch housing wasn't made to be taken apart, for instance. Among the broken pieces I found a burned-out contact that couldn't be repaired anyway. But for $1.15 I bought a replacement switch that can carry more current than the original.

One thing leads to another. Coming home from the hardware store, I strolled down an alley behind a grocery and picked up a useful wooden box—and two beautiful tomatoes and an onion. Of course, a little glop had to be washed off to bring out their beauty. So a tomato (minus a bruised spot) and the onion (minus a moldy spot) went into the curry I made for lunch. As I ate, a crew pulled up in front to cut dead limbs from two eucalyptus trees on the city's esplanade. I hustled out with work gloves and axe, offering to take the wood off their hands. They cut it to fireplace length and I split it on the spot.

That was quite a day. Besides life and health and home and family to thank God for, I had a useful vacuum cleaner (for $1.15), expanded knowledge of electricity and mechanics (no tuition charge), a cubic yard of fireplace wood for the winter (delivered free), plus several examples for this piece on recycling. And my recycled lunch would have brought praise from gourmets (especially if they didn't know the source of some of the ingredients).

In principle, recycling isn't far removed from the biblical ideas of redemption, salvation and regeneration. You might say that Christians are spiritually recycled people. Jesus Christ said he came for the "lost," the "least" and the "last." Through him the lost among us would be saved. The least would become greatest in God's kingdom. The last to merit human consideration would be first to find favor with his Father.

When sinful humanity began to mess up this beautiful planet he gave us for a home, the Creator didn't toss us into the cosmic garbage can and say "good riddance." He saw the potential in wasted, wasteful people. He sent Jesus Christ to redeem us, to give us "new life" at the cost of his own. Because of that divine process, including his resurrection, all Christians care about "human ecology." Knowing that God designed people to be like himself, to last forever, we think of any wasted human life as a tragedy. So the most important task in the world is to help people find new life in Christ.

Christians give a lot of thought to evangelism in an effort to "recycle" the human spirit. We don't want to be distracted from that. But additional thought and effort could also redeem the human environment. Recycling material things does take a certain amount of our time. But practice at it teaches us to use more effectively whatever God gives us, including time.

Recycling takes a certain amount of space, too. We hunted for a big old house with room for storage and a workshop, even though we had little to furnish it with. Now our house is full of "treasures," each with its story: where we found it, who it once belonged to, how it was made. Recycling teaches us how to use space efficiently: storing small boxes inside of larger ones, creating sensible categories and so on. To make good use of something in the future, we have to put it where we can find it and where it won't deteriorate. Some people compulsively save leftover food and then let it rot.

Recycling teaches selectivity. There are hierarchies of use-fulness. Some worn shirts are worth mending for wear in public. Others are best to wear when painting. Some are good only for rags. But any shirt has some use left in it.

Taking care of things keeps them in the highest categories of usefulness. If you use a chisel to open paint cans, you've lost a woodcarving tool. Clean rags have more uses than dirty ones. We rinse out all milk cartons to keep them from smell-ing sour. Clean, they can be used for all kinds of things: can-dle molds, berry-picking baskets, containers for kitchen waste, planters. At the end of the line, surplus milk cartons full of twigs or squashed flat make superb fire starters.

I've stressed the private benefits of recycling, like econ-omy and education. Public benefits are just as important but not so easy to demonstrate or agree on. Friends of the earth sometimes agree on goals but disagree on strategy. Denomi-nations crop up in ecology as well as theology: you find both "conservationists" and "preservationists." Well, dying people can't wait until churches settle all their theological differences. We have to get on with presenting Christ. A dying earth can't wait for unanimity either.

It's more important to begin recycling than to do every-thing right at first. The Shortney paperback *How to Live on Nothing* is enough to get you started. You can pick up more ideas from *The Mother Earth News* and articles on ecology.

One thing holds a lot of us back. It's a feeling that our puny effort doesn't amount to much, with industrial pollution and waste rampant. Christians seldom react that way about evan-gelism. We witness because we care about individuals, what-ever is happening to the world's population. It's true that the cumulative effect of human rebellion against God is awful to contemplate. It has put such scars on the environment that "the whole creation has been groaning," longing to be set free (Rom. 8:18-25).

Well, even if we can't liberate the whole creation, maybe

we can clean up some of the mess. Our Lord seemed to care about small things, children and sparrows and such. Beginnings are always small, but let's begin.

SOMEWHERE BETWEEN—Reflections Five Years Later: Walter Hearn

In 1971 I was a research scientist and tenured professor at Iowa State University. I was doing the most satisfying work I could imagine getting paid to do, and I was paid so well that I was sometimes embarrassed to be enjoying my work so much. I was forty-five. The next year I gave up my university job and, as far as my colleagues were concerned, "dropped out of the system."

I had put twenty years as a Ph.D. into my profession, into several academic communities and into the lives of countless individual students. I worked among congenial and intelligent people in a parklike campus setting with an atmosphere of freedom and integrity. Unlike many dropouts I've met since, I had no bitterness or resentment toward the establishment. I praise God for the opportunities it afforded me. Until 1972, I was sure that's where he wanted me to be.

By that time I had also put in some thirty-five years as a Christian. I had responded to the preaching of the gospel and given my life to Jesus Christ before I entered high school.[17] I learned to pray and to listen to God's leading. He led me into a scientific career, possibly because I had too much imagination for some lines of work and not enough for others.[18]

Now I believe he has led me out of that career into something new. To some, that seems very "radical." Is it? *Everything* was once new to me: science, scholarship, how to live as a follower of Jesus. As a young Christian I took the Bible as my sourcebook and guidebook. But because I've never seen it as a handbook or "cookbook," I've had to count on God to guide me, through his Holy Spirit. He has a knack for blending biblical insights, circumstances and the counsel of others into a spiritual conviction strong enough to overcome my innate caution and scientist's skepticism.

Why I "dropped out." Probably because this career change was so irreversible, and because my resilience isn't what it used to be, the Lord took the trouble to cumulate a half-dozen arguments for taking such a risk.

First, God convinced me that he had something important for me to do. Young people sometimes drop out and then just "hang out." They quit school or whatever they're doing merely because "it's a drag," with no vision of anything else worth giving themselves to. I was more like Thoreau: "I left the woods for as good a reason as I went there. Perhaps it seemed to me that I had several more lives to live, and could not spare any more time for that one."[19] I had always had a love for words and an interest in writing. I had tested in various ways what I hoped was a gift for using words. Besides scientific papers I had published book reviews, magazine articles and chapters in books. I did writing jobs nobody else in my department wanted, including a weekly newsletter I began and edited for ten years. In my spare-time writing, the interaction of science and Christian faith was a frequent theme. I discovered I had more to say on that subject than spare time in which to say it. My wife, an experienced editor whose opinion I valued, was convinced that I should write more. (She was also convinced that it's impossible or at least extremely difficult to earn a living solely from writing.)

Second, God probed my conscience with some ethical questions about what I was doing with my life. Those questions weren't the heavy ones raised by "big science" or "technocracy." I wasn't working on weaponry or nuclear power or genetic manipulation. Most of my work was "pure" research vaguely related to medicine or agriculture. Generally the problems I investigated were chosen to train future scientists. Eventually, even that benign policy began to get to me. "How long can that go on?" I asked. "Where will their research money come from? And what if I have trained them to enjoy repeating the process, training more graduate students, who in turn will train more, and so on? Resources are limited on our planet, and who has the right to do more than reproduce himself? Is it really society's needs that demand the training of more scientists in our image—or is it the demands of our own egos?"[20]

I realized, of course, that even if I became a professional writer I would face as many ethical problems as I faced as a professional scientist. But they would be different. I had grappled with one set of problems and learned how to pray for those who face them daily. Maybe the Lord wanted me to bring Christian faith to bear on a new set of problems, to cope with new temptations, to witness in a new environment.

Third, God gave me a sense that a phase of my life had come to completion. Anyone in whom God's Spirit is active should expect to change with time. Even if we didn't change, circumstances would. Christians should be sensitive to God's timing and know when he wants us to move. I didn't want to stay on, doing more of the same, just to build up a comfortable retirement annuity. The number of Christian faculty on my campus had been increasing, so the witness to students and to other professors would continue without me. I had left my mark on the place, trying to humanize the bureaucracy in various ways, and realized I could make a new kind of contribution simply by resigning. My department could replace me with a woman or a black, or at least with some young Ph.D. hungry for work in a tight job market.

For many scientists, science is their whole life, or at least the center of it. I was one of the few who could walk away from it. Christ was the center of my life.

Fourth, God was nurturing in me a desire for simplicity and wholeness in life. Concentration on science or any other highly specialized occupation leads to fragmentation. In my daily work I could be something of a generalist in teaching but had to be a specialist in research. For a long time research was fun, but I was becoming more of a research administrator, and I lacked any ambition to keep going at that. At the beginning of most establishment careers, hard work often gets you out from under most of the people over you, and thus leads toward freedom and wholeness. But after a certain point, more hard work only puts you on top of more people. That was not for me. The only alternative I could think of was the route taken by creative artists, who seldom work in a hierarchy at any level—at least until imminent starvation forces them to take a regular job.

Not wanting to "get ahead" but also not wanting merely to "get by," I thought it must be time to "get out" and "get busy" at a new creative task. I wanted to simplify my life along with my work, to find a "lifework" of wholeness. I hadn't yet thought of simple living as a Christian obligation in the light of economic injustice, but I was beginning to see it as an ecological necessity. Yet I still had questions. How many people can be artists, writers or small entrepreneurs? Realistically, doesn't scarcity of resources demand the efficiency of big business? Is it cowardly to try to escape what the overwhelming majority of people have to endure?

Fifth, God was focusing more of my attention on my family. Ginny and I needed to unify, as well as to simplify, our life together. We knew that the biblical priority is God first, family second, and occupation third, but we saw that priority continually challenged by a husband's demanding occupation. I had drawn my wife into some areas of my work, such as opening our home to students. I helped in the kitchen and she helped me with office work, but there was no way she could enter into things of great importance to me if I devoted myself to a profession for which she wasn't trained. And what about her profession? We wanted to work together at major tasks, to share a profession. It seemed clear that I could enter her profession easier than she could enter mine.

Also, the Lord had brought into our lives the disaffected teen-age sons and daughters of some busy colleagues. They showed us where our own children might be. headed. We started opening up our family to others, and thinking of the family as the focal point of our Christian ministry.

Sixth, God kept alive in me a reasonably adventurous spirit and an interest in testing alternatives. Those years in the lab had taught me something about how to experiment. I had the curiosity and a kind of cautious courage to see if we could find another way to live. I knew other Christians who were dissatisfied with their conventional lives, but who didn't think that any other way was "practical." To experiment with my own life was a way of using my training and experience to benefit the church as a whole. If, with God's help, I could find "another way," others might be encouraged to try. If I failed, others would know better.

So the arguments went, piling up until they tipped the scales. Personal factors entered the mix, especially during frigid Iowa winters when my southern corpuscles, circulating through pedal extremities, froze to corpsicles. I longed for salubrity, but we wanted to be where the Lord wanted us even if that meant staying in Ames, Iowa. We thought we should be in a university town, so we considered three others: Austin, Fayetteville and Berkeley. We had spent a year's leave in Berkeley and loved it, but were afraid that with its high cost of living it was no place to serve a writer's apprenticeship. The other two were warmer than Ames but cheaper than Berkeley. And there was a further good possibility we could buy the home we were renting in Ames and not have the expense of moving at all. As a writer, I could always hibernate!

At the end of December, 1971, I went off the payroll and waited to see what would happen. We prayed a lot.

What happened. At first nothing—except sickening uncertainty. Waiting for geographical directions, we wondered if we had already misread the signs. Had we made a terrible mistake? After letting us stew for three months, the Lord served up a miracle in the form of the perfect house for us in Berkeley. We had enough savings for the down payment, but with no salary we looked like poor risks for a loan. We hadn't even thought of that, having always been employed. But the Lord knew we needed a house, so we got the loan.

Medical insurance at low-cost group rates was something else we had taken for granted. Having no medical insurance made Ginny nervous, but even the Berkeley Co-op group plan was too expensive. Instead we now make use of some excellent free clinics and so far we've been able to keep a cushion of savings as our private "group medical insurance." Small group, big risk; but no one can insure against everything that conceivably might happen—especially in earthquake country.

After exemptions and deductions and business expenses were subtracted from our miscellaneous bits of income, we found ourselves in a zero tax bracket. During Vietnam war years I wrote an annual letter with our federal income tax return, protesting that if our government kept bombing people, we intended to stop paying for the bombs. With our 1972 return I could write: "See, I warned you." In those first years we watched our savings dwindle and our sources of income keep changing. None of them has ever been very secure.

I get a small monthly income for editing the Newsletter of the American Scientific Affiliation (ASA) and Ginny gets even less for copy editing *Radix* for the Berkeley Christian Coalition. But the Lord has been imaginative in finding other work for us. Our first year, U.C. Berkeley needed someone to teach a biochemistry course one quarter. The next summer I filled in at Regent College in Vancouver, B.C., teaching a course on science and Christianity. That honorarium was exactly enough to replace our 1966 VW engine, which blew on the trip home. Without becoming cocky, we were developing confidence that God would provide. When the university asked me to teach again, I cut the last strand of our economic umbilical cord: I turned them down to get on with what God had called us to do.

More of my time has gone into editing, which I learned from Ginny, than into writing. In another perfectly timed miracle, the Lord opened up editorial work for us almost before we began seeking it. In the next three years we edited around fifty books for Christian and secular publishers and a number of doctoral dissertations and shorter manuscripts. We're always alert for new income possibilities.

Ironically, it seems almost as hard to find time for writing now as before. We're convinced that God has given us a ministry of hospitality with our wonderful old house, so we feed lots of people and open our home to others in need of shelter for short periods of time. Such a practice ungraciously wars against solitude. As frugal as we are with money, we sometimes spend our time quite extravagantly. Good investments of time have included: seminars for young Christian writers; Crucible, the Berkeley Christian Coalition's free university; the house church that began in our living room; and corresponding with many people whom the Lord loves and listening to others.

Our hope of working together has been fulfilled in a remarkable way. We share the kitchen work and other tasks of hospitality. Now that I edit books with Ginny, we do better work as a team than either could do alone. Ginny gets great satisfaction out of providing as much income as I do and was the first of us to produce a book. A second book she has since put together portrays the struggles of Christian women to move from second-class citizenship to full participation in the church and the world.[21]

Together, we're trying not only to share each other's roles in marriage, but also to change sexist patterns in the church and society. The church and the secular world alike foster selfishness and pride in men by valuing their gifts above those of women and looking almost solely to men for leadership. We think that a husband's contribution ought not to be evaluated apart from that of his wife. His contribution and hers should be added together and divided by two. I'm proud that my contribution would be enhanced, not diminished, by such a procedure.

The profound changes in the way we live have been easier because we haven't made them alone. We never expected to drag a lot of people along with us, but we have found others whom God is leading in the same direction. Many people here in Berkeley, mostly younger than we are, try to live simply and creatively. Others around the country whom we know through correspondence or their writings form a supportive network. Our own writings have encouraged others. "A Journey toward Simplicity" (which we had titled merely "Another Way") has been widely reprinted.[22] It and the material on recycling[23] plus an interview formed the basis for a 1975 article about the changes in our life in the Los Angeles Times. To our surprise, that story was picked up by major newspapers all over the country and by the nationally circulated tabloid Moneysworth.[24] Our Christian motivation came through clearly, but not our productive labors. The Times story was headlined "Ph.D. Scrounges for a Living." It's true that we're not too proud to use what others throw away, but we don't want to give the impression that we've thrown our lives away.

Middle-aged and middle-classified. Our unexpected notoriety has made us aware that to most middle-class Americans we look like revolutionaries. A couple of years ago an ASA member wrote that someone who knew me in the past "thinks you're a fanatic and are wasting your talent as an academician and researcher." He must have read that Times article.

Once when Ginny and I were speaking to a church group about how we live, we got a decidedly negative response. We were listing some practical ways we've cut our spending, so we can live on less than half of our previous income and still give money to Christian causes. One of our principles, to "stay out of stores as much as possible," upset one man in particular. He owned a store. "If everyone lived your way," he came back at us, "the American economy would collapse." But when everyone lives "the American way," materials are depleted so rapidly that the whole world heads for disaster.

Yet, to some Berkeley young people, we look not like revolutionaries but like the bourgeoisie. After all, we have preserved our family structure, live in a nice neighborhood, are paying off a mortgage, still have some savings and a car, work for the "establishment" whenever we can get free-lance editorial work, and are relatively dispassionate about politics. Although we believe in trimming the power of the privileged and relieving the plight of the poor through political action, I doubt that in the eyes of some we could ever become poor enough or radical enough to "escape the middle class." I'm not even sure I want to. I think I'd rather be somewhere between rich and poor. Isn't that where even Marxists want everybody to be? When extreme wealth and extreme poverty are both eliminated, society will be "classless." In other words, everybody will be in one universal class—where the middle used to be.

Why is the "middle class" looked down on? Because middle-class values are largely commercial values. Most advertising is aimed at influencing middle-class people or at stimulating desire in poorer people for middle-class luxuries. Hence, irresponsible consumerism is regarded as a middle-class characteristic even though the very rich are more conspicuously extravagant. Further, since materialistic preoccupation dulls aesthetic sensibilities, poor taste is a middle-class characteristic in the eyes of the wealthy or intellectually inclined.

Of course I don't want my life to be characterized by either overconsumption or "plastic culture." But a middle-class heritage need not hinder spiritual or moral leadership. One advantage of people in the middle is that we generally have stamina and stability. We're not so egregiously tempted to live carelessly, as are both the rich and the poor. The very rich can afford waste because they have more than they need. The desperately poor, believing they can never be anything else, often doubt that taking care of things or investing their lives for long-range goals is worth the effort.

Frugality is the way most of us, or our parents or grandparents, got into the middle class in the first place. Saving for the future, building durable institutions, managing our lives, conserving resources—that's what we ought to be good at. To take a "middle of the road" position means to play it safe, to hang on to what is worth keeping. What's wrong with that, as long as it's really worth keeping?

So, what should we do if we're middle-classified, especially if we've grown all the way into middle age that way? First, let's recognize that there's nothing wrong with a middle position. The Bible commends peacemaking, which can be done only in the middle, between two antagonists. We're to stay in the thick of it—in the world but uncontaminated by the world. Christians are to be joyful (that is, creative) and responsible (that is, redemptive) individuals. To me, *joyful* means somewhere between the foolishness of the rich and the grimness of the poor. *Responsible* means somewhere between the respectable and the radical, between laissez-faireism and bloody revolt.

There's a lot of room between feeling that we can't make any significant changes in the system and feeling that we have to change everything. The fact is that we can change *some* things. Ginny and I have made some changes in our life. Those changes have helped others make changes. Change has been set in motion.

If you're a middle-class Christian but vaguely uneasy about it, open yourself up to new possibilities. There are excellent books[25] and periodicals[26] to raise your consciousness about stewardship, ecological responsibility and economic justice, and to suggest practical steps to take. Share those ideas cautiously with others who are already awake or who've slept long enough.

Take a few small steps toward living more creatively and redemptively. Even one small step toward less consumption, taken quietly and deliberately in the Lord's name, starts changing things in the right direction. Walk somewhere instead of using your car; eat simpler and more nutritious foods; drink hot water with a little milk in it ("pearl tea") instead of expensive coffee; recycle something; begin to compost kitchen wastes for a vegetable garden; buy secondhand instead of new—there are a thousand ways to begin. One step leads to another, especially when a few like-minded people reinforce each other. Soon you may have more money to give to good causes,[27] more opportunity to share, more satisfaction from working together at something worthwhile, maybe even less need for a high-status, high-paying job.

A Parable. A Middle-Class Family once encountered a Radical Christian who had jetted to California from Elsewhere. Across his secondhand surfboard was written, in large block letters, the word REPENT. Perceiving him to be a Prophet not in his own country, they honored him. Since he had come to write a book, they offered him board and a quiet room in exchange for a bit of "serfing" around their old run-down house. The book was to be a devastating exposé of American middle-class Christianity, he said.

In a few weeks, however, he moved out. He joined a group of Young People in a Commune, which, by what he called the New Hermeneutics, had become the More Biblical Way. The people in the Middle Class Family could see that their house was not a good place for a Prophet to write a book. But after he moved out they kept hoping he would finish it, partly out of curiosity. They wondered if they were in it. Meanwhile, they stayed in the Middle Class. That may be where they belong.

To paraphrase the late Berkeley folksinger Malvina Reynolds (composer of "Little Boxes"), Ginny and I often feel that:

Somewhere between the rich and the radical,
Somewhere between the weak and the strong,
Somewhere between the fat and the lean,
Somewhere between—is where we belong.[28]

AN EFFORT TO CHANGE LIFESTYLE: Howard H. Claassen
If changes in lifestyle are being contemplated that will reduce our comfortable affluence, our incentives will have to come from biblical principles. Four goals seem to me to be biblically based.

The first is to learn to understand the poor by lessening the large economic gap between us and them. The vast majority of the people in the world are very poor. God loves the poor and frequently states his special concern for them in the Bible.

A second goal is to try to avoid materialism, the love of possessions and money. That one is tricky. To live frugally and place a large fraction of our income into savings will not do. That savings account may feed our materialism rather than starve it.

A third goal is to reduce consumption of resources that are scarce and nonrenewable and to reduce pollution of the environment. That involves conservation and recycling of waste materials.

A fourth goal is to reduce causes of international tensions and wars. Does our country possess the world's strongest military force because we are concerned about protecting the rights of poor and oppressed people or because we feel the need to protect our freedom to buy resources cheaply in all parts of the world? Probably the second reason is the honest one, and so I should, at least, reduce my own contribution to our country's pattern of consumption of resources.

In our home we have made changes based on these principles. Our progress is not exemplary, and of course the needs of each family are unique. We are a family of two, our children having moved to other cities. Some of our choices are limited because my wife, Esther, is in poor health. Bicycling, for example, is not possible for her.

For us, living frugally has generally been relatively easy. Driving a ten-year-old car seems quite satisfactory to both of us. But when our children had finished college, and lower expenses on their behalf allowed us to save money, we began to see the increasing danger of materialism. We decided that the regular payroll deductions for retirement were adequate and that we should not put additional money into savings. Giving up some less-than-necessary expenditure was meaningful in our lives only if the money saved would actually be given away. So we began to give away the portion of income that was above our needs. Even with only my salary from a Christian college, it turned out that our giving approached fifty percent of our take-home pay (our home was paid for).

After two years of that we developed an alternate plan. The six years left before my reaching retirement age would be divided into two periods: three years with salary and three years in another place, where we would serve without salary. We are now in the second year of this plan and are praying for God's direction to his place of service for the latter three years. Now for a few specific examples in our lifestyle.

For transportation to and from my job (seven miles total) I use a bicycle. In bad weather, I ride in a car pool with two others. The bicycle is handy for running errands, and I never have a parking problem. When Esther goes along we use the car, but we plan our trips carefully to combine several errands if possible. Although begun because of the energy crisis, my bicycling has become an enjoyable part of my day.

For many years we have avoided paying for garbage pickup. Our cans and bottles are recycled, and most organic wastes go to our garden. A week's supply of junk mail burned in our stove will heat up a room nicely. Burying kitchen garbage to feed worms is more fun than allowing it to go smelly while waiting for the garbage truck. Our soil has become richer while also growing a large fraction of our vegetables. If most people did this, the gasoline the garbage trucks use could be saved.

We heat only those rooms where we are actually present; a 55° bedroom with blankets provides good sleeping.

We do not buy meats and other foods that seem expensive. That limits our meat primarily to chicken and to bargain turkey drumsticks. As for eating out, that is rare. We generally avoid group dinners that cost more than $3.50 (with an occasional exception for me for professional reasons).

In general, the simple lifestyle takes time. It can mean more time for family members to work together, and that has been valuable. It is too easy for one's professional activities to take one away from the family. On the other hand, a person cannot, I think, accomplish as much professionally if he or she helps to can tomatoes, dry apples and so on. That may be a negative factor, but many of us probably overestimate the importance of our own professional accomplishments.

When trying to simplify your lifestyle, I think it is important to have support from one's Christian community. In our case, we find a good bit of support among the college faculty.

OUR CURRENT WALK WITH GOD: Douglas and Margaret Feaver

Lifestyle seems an inappropriate word to describe our approach to life as Christians. It is inappropriate not merely because it is a fashionable buzz word in non-Christian circles, but because of its connotations: of a variety of options, all equally valid, differentiated by inconsequential vagaries of style and fashion—like a choice of color schemes, for example.

As Christians we have given up our rights to choose, to indulge our preferences or to follow our fancies. We have committed ourselves to lives pleasing to the One who has bought us and owns us and has the right to order our consumption patterns.

Thus we cannot really pinpoint any "move toward a simple lifestyle" since we have always felt that the Lord would provide all that was necessary for us to accomplish his purposes in our lives. Whether those things were "simple" or "complicated" was his business, not ours. Here are some major elements in our current walk:

1. *Debt.* It is our practice not to borrow any money, not to "owe anyone anything, except love." The one exception is the mortgage on our home, where the debt payments are considerably lower than any rent payments would be. Our house is in a modest neighborhood where we can walk to school, church and job.

2. *Work.* We have only one salary, since Margaret, although a qualified R.N., has felt called to full-time homemaking and ministries in and through the home. As the children grow up, this may change, but for the time being it is the way we live. God has so supplied that until now Margaret has not "had to get out to work" to make ends meet.

3. *Things.* We have never had television in our home. Our stereos have been homemade kits or inexpensive models. On the other hand, we have some fine musical instruments and we and the children often use them for personal pleasure and to minister to others. Our furniture and furnishings are modest, our cars (we have two) are inexpensive subcompacts

without the "options." We have no objections to wearing secondhand clothing from more affluent brothers and sisters.

I usually walk to work (two miles each way) and carry a brown-bag lunch. We have largely given up steak and roast beef for family meals, but enjoy a varied and nutritious menu.

Vacations have emphasized camping. In connection with my work, the family has come with me to Europe, where we lived and traveled within our salary budget for the period, without dipping into savings.

4. *Giving.* Our tithe has from the beginning been a full ten percent off the "before taxes" salary figure. In addition, we put honoraria for messages given at Christian gatherings in a special account which becomes our "offerings" in addition to our tithe. The tithes and offerings are given to the church, missions, appeals for relief and so forth. We also give some money directly when we know of special need. All our giving is not necessarily covered by tax deductions.

Following the Lord has not always been easy, and many times we have been tempted to indulge ourselves or our children more, but we wholeheartedly affirm that ours has been a happy and healthy life.

We would not advocate copying our family model. Rather, we would encourage all Christians to explore their personal life patterns in accordance with principles in God's Word.

OUR PILGRIMAGE IN SIMPLICITY: Art and Peggy Gish

We never have really made a decision to move toward a simpler lifestyle. We were both raised in homes where we had little money and lived frugally. We had little money in college, so we lived quite simply. One of our important decisions was that after school we would continue to live simply.

We are very grateful for that decision. It has not only saved us a lot of frenzy, wasted life and inauthentic living, but has helped open many doors to exciting alternatives. What we are doing is no sacrifice. To do anything else would be the sacrifice.

Living simply has taken more than one form for us. We have lived in the city, in suburbia and now on a farm. We lived this way before we had children, and now with three children. We have lived as an independent family, and now in a covenant community.

It is important to recognize that our focus must always be Jesus and his kingdom. Our lifestyle is just an expression of that focus. Whenever we put lifestyle concerns in the center the result is works-righteousness and legalism. But we also recognize that living in the kingdom has little meaning if it is not fleshed out in our lifestyles.

An essential aspect of our lifestyle now is being part of New Covenant Fellowship, a small Christian community in which we have felt called to live out our commitment to God's kingdom through mutual submission to our brothers and sisters. That includes not only community of goods, but also sharing all the important decisions of our lives. We are learning what it means to give up control of our own lives and future and to trust God and our brothers and sisters. It is not easy, however.

Our community provides a loving atmosphere for our children, including our own school and the opportunity for the children to share in our lives as we work, play, sing and serve each other. We feel no need for television. We are grateful for common work, the chance to worship together each day and the daily support and challenge. We all want our attitudes and lifestyles to be molded by God's kingdom, in which we are called to live now.

An important part of our life together is seeking to bring our economic lives into conformity with the standards of biblical justice. That means we have to seek concretely to identify our lives with the poor, to live simply, to consume less of the world's resources, to rely more on renewable sources of energy and to work for social justice. That, we feel, must begin with us, but it cannot stop with us.

It has not been easy to discern where to draw lines, how much is enough, and when it makes sense to spend more time in order to use less resources. Our lifestyle has meant a lot of extra work, less leisure time to do the things we want and less individual independence. It has taken a fair amount of time to come to decisions on how much cheese and meat to eat, how much to use automobiles and how our concern for the poor should relate to how we earn the little money we need.

We are grateful that those decisions do not have to be made independently by our family, but are shared with others with similar commitments. Although each family in our community is very important, we are also part of a larger body and it is in that body that our family life takes shape.

Although we believe that no one particular form of lifestyle is intended for all Christians, we feel the urgency for the lifestyle of all Christians to take the particular form that God intends for them—and that it be concrete and specific, molded by God's Spirit and not by the spirit and structures of this present age.

For families and individuals who desire to live a more faithful lifestyle and be more discerning in their economic lives, we have the following suggestions.

1. Begin to make all your decisions in relation to Jesus and God's will for your lives. Allow Jesus actually to be the Lord and norm of your lives. Spend more time praying about the decisions you face.

2. Begin to share all your important decisions with Christian brothers and sisters in community and together discern what God's will is for those decisions.

3. Begin to identify your lives with the poor. Before buying or using anything, ask yourselves what that action means

in relationship to the reality of poverty and starvation. Ask how your lifestyle contributes to or is based on injustice.

4. Begin to consider how your actions affect the environment. Ask how your actions contribute to pollution, destruction of the land and depletion of the world's resources. Ask whether your lifestyle is ecologically responsible.

A MODEST EFFORT AT LIVING MORE SIMPLY:
Carol Westphal

A friend and I were talking together over lunch recently. The subject: simple living. "My husband," said she, "thinks simple living means no new clothes for the next two years. But I told him I couldn't stand looking at him for two years without new clothes. I suggested we give up going out to dinner, but he said, 'No way! I need that.' So you see our dilemma." I do.

Simple living is an individual matter: a person choosing before God how best to be a steward of his gifts in today's world of such gross inequalities. To try to spell out how our family responds frightens me, as I am so conscious of the tendency to legalize. Perhaps we're too sophisticated for legalism, but at least it's hard not to begin comparing standards of living and vying for the position of "simplest of all" or at least "simpler than thou"—trying to keep *down* with the Smiths or the Joneses.

My husband and I have always been of fairly frugal mind, but our commitment to simple living has meant some steps beyond frugality. We came to that understanding as we became increasingly aware of the gap between rich and poor in our world, of the relation between our wealth and their poverty, and of the biblical teaching about God's people and how we should live together. For a time we struggled very much on our own in wealthy Westchester County (New York). We felt no call to join a community; instead we believed ourselves to be where God wanted us, but we longed for the sup-

port of other Christians. Since moving to Holland (Michigan)
we have been blessed as a family with many friends in our
local church whose values are similar to our own. Their
specifics are undoubtedly different, but we share the basic
convictions that (1) material goods are gifts from God to be
shared and not to be hoarded; and (2) there is much more to
life than just the material side. For those friends and their
supportive presence we are grateful.

Now, what has "worked" for us as a family? We quickly
found that it is difficult to live simply if one has too much
money. So the first thing we have done is to adopt something
similar to Ron Sider's "graduated tithe." We have never developed his "base line," but as our salary has increased, we
have periodically reviewed the percentage of our giving and
increased it, thus reducing or leveling our standard of living,
rather than constantly raising it.

That practice has led to a number of important decisions
for our family. For example, when it came to purchasing a
home in Holland after selling the one in New York, it was
tempting to opt for another one that was within our salary
range and had a distinctive aura of elegance. Instead, we
chose a home that was considerably plainer and would not
eat up so much in monthly mortgage payments. No sympathy, please. Our plainer house is a far cry from poverty;
nevertheless, the choice for us was significant.

Similarly with a car. When our old car had told us in no
uncertain terms that it would not drive us through one more
Michigan winter, we sympathized. For our new vehicle, we
chose a cut-down version that gives our family all the togeth-
erness we could ask for—but is adequate. Again, not a radical
decision, to be sure, but for us another reminder that our lives
must be understood and lived in a growing awareness of hungry brothers and sisters.

We have not made any hard-line rules about new clothes,
toys, books and so on. We try, again, to be cautious and let

our needs, rather than our wants, govern our choices. For the children with their toys this has sometimes been difficult. But we've found at least two things that help. First, we've tried to create in our children an awareness of advertising pressures, helping them to understand how TV advertising affects all of us. We often question commercials together and frequently laugh at their claims. That has given our kids some distance from advertising pressures and has also helped them to be more self-conscious about "created wants." Second, in the last few years we have developed a Christmas custom that holds down our spending and adds a new dimension to the holiday as well. We add up the cost of our family gifts and place a check under the Christmas tree of comparable value, to be sent to a development project abroad. The children have responded well to this idea of getting a little less and sharing a little more.

In the area of recreation and family fun, we have tried to choose activities that are available to all people and are as cost-free as possible. We are spoiled, I admit, with a beautiful new gymnasium and swimming pool at Hope College, which we thoroughly enjoy together. Camping is something we pondered for many years, not at all sure we could hack the muss and fuss. As of this summer, we have joined the ranks of campers, purchasing a tent that will be shared with a family from our church.

Of course we consciously keep our thermostat down, walk or bike when possible, use as few appliances as possible, but our most frequent reminder that we are trying to live simply is our diet. We fight the junk-food battle constantly (we win some and lose some), avoid processed foods and try to limit intake. We've joined a food cooperative, and we eat lots of soup and few desserts. We have also tried meat cutbacks, substituting alternative protein sources lower on the food chain. About twice a week I try to serve a delectable and colorful meatless meal. One evening I enthusiastically pre-

sented my husband Merold and the children a gourmet delight—zucchini souffle. Our seven-year-old son sniffed and
poked at his portion while I cheerily asked if someone could
explain why we were having a meatless meal. Said he, with a
heavy sigh, "Cause this is what the poor people have to eat?"
Occasionally, when it all seems too heavy, we hop in the car
and have a conscience-lapse at McDonald's!

I think simpler living has been a meaningful experience
for us as a family. I cannot claim we have felt the freedom and
exhilaration some talk about. For us, it is often a struggle.
Decisions are constantly facing us that I often wish would go
away. I don't mean to sound grim—just realistic. We have
gained as a family, if not exhilaration, then a deep sense of
joy in sharing with our whole lives in God's kingdom work.
We have known a greater communion with those who live
simply not because they choose to, but because they must.

Notes

[1]Shakertown Pledge Group. c/o Friends Meeting House, W. 44th and
York South, Minneapolis, Minn. 55410.

[2]John V. Taylor, *Enough is Enough* (London: SCM Press, 1975).

[3]Amitai Etzioni, "The Family: Is it Obsolete?" in *Journal of Current
Social Issues*, 14 (Feb. 1977), pp. 4-9.

[4]Phil Amerson, "Lifestyle Research: A Review of Resources," in *Review of Religious Research*, 20 (Summer 1979), p. 353.

[5]Virginia Satir, *Peoplemaking* (Palo Alto, Calif.: Science and Behavior
Books, Inc., 1972), p. 3.

[6]Walter Brueggemann, "The Covenanted Family: A Zone for Human-
ness," in *Journal of Current Social Issues*, 14 (Feb. 1977), p. 23.

[7]Available as a pamphlet from Mennonite Central Committee, 21 South
12th Street, Akron, Pa. 12501.

[8]This statement is an adaptation of articles originally appearing in
Radix magazine, Box 4307, Berkeley, Calif. 94704.

[9]John Wesley quoted in Max Weber, *Sociology of Religion* (Boston:
Beacon Press, 1963), p. 175.

[10]*The Last Whole Earth Catalog* (Menlo Park: Portola Institute, 1971), pp.
24-25.

[11]*Black Bart*, Nov. 1971, pp. 15-20.

[12]Reprinted in William James, *Memories and Studies* (New York: Longmans, Green & Co., 1911).

[13]*The Variorum Walden,* ed. Walter Harding (New York: Washington Square Press, 1962), pp. 1-58.

[14]*Journal of a Walden Two Commune* (Louisa, Va.: Twin Oaks Community, 1972).

[15]*How to Live on Nothing* (New York: Pocket Books, 1968), p. xi.

[16]*Living Poor with Style* (New York: Bantam Books, 1972), p. 311.

[17]See *What They Did Right: Reflections on Parents by Their Children,* ed. Virginia Hearn (Wheaton, Ill.: Tyndale, 1974), pp. 97-107.

[18]See "A Biochemist Shares His Faith," in *Why I Am Still a Christian,* ed. E. M. Blaiklock (Grand Rapids, Mich.: Zondervan, 1971), pp. 65-80.

[19]Harding, p. 244.

[20]"Whole People and Half Truths," in *The Scientist and Ethical Decision,* ed. Charles Hatfield (Downers Grove, Ill.: InterVarsity Press, 1973), p. 89.

[21]*Our Struggle to Serve,* ed. Virginia Hearn (Waco, Tex.: Word, 1979).

[22]Walter and Ginny Hearn, "Another Way," *Radix* (then called *Right On*), May 1973.

[23]Walt Hearn, "The Whole Creation Groans," *Radix* (then called *Right On*), January 1974.

[24]Russell Chandler, "Ph.D. Scrounges for a Living," *Los Angeles Times,* 1 December 1975, Part I, p. 3; "Brainy Couple Goes for Broke to Break with Wasteful U.S. Lifestyle," *Moneysworth,* 15 March 1976, p. 13.

[25]For example: Arthur G. Gish, *Beyond the Rat Race* (Scottdale, Pa.: Herald Press, 1973); Richard K. Taylor, *Economics and the Gospel* (Philadelphia: Union Church Press, 1973); John V. Taylor, *Enough is Enough* (London: SCM Press, 1975); Arthur Simon, *Bread for the World* (Grand Rapids, Mich.: Eerdmans, 1975); Jim Wallis, *Agenda for Biblical People* (New York: Harper & Row, 1976); Ronald J. Sider, *Rich Christians in an Age of Hunger* (Downers Grove, Ill.: InterVarsity Press, 1977).

[26]Besides Berkeley Christian Coalition's *Radix,* try: *The Other Side* (300 W. Apsley, Box 12236, Philadelphia, Pa. 19144); a new Christian public affairs newsletter put out by Christians for Urban Justice (598 Columbia Rd., Dorchester, Mass. 02125); and the newsletter of Bread for the World (207 E. 16th St., New York, N.Y. 10003).

[27]A modest proposal by Ronald J. Sider for Christians to start giving beyond their tithe appears in *The Graduated Tithe* (Downers Grove, Ill.: InterVarsity Press, 1978), a reprint of chapter seven of *Rich Christians in an Age of Hunger.*

[28]Paraphrased from "Somewhere Between" on the record album *Malvina,* Cassandra Records. The original words, about being both sinner and saint, are copyrighted by Shroder Music Company (ASCAP).

STRUGGLING FREE IN THE CHURCH: GUIDELINES AND MODELS

5

Local congregations, like individual families, are searching for specific models for living more simply. The churches described in this chapter are all trying to do that, each in their own way in their own unique context. From his setting in the black evangelical church, Michael E. Haynes offers some provoking questions and suggestions for all churches interested in a corporate ecclesiastical lifestyle consistent with our worship of the God revealed in Scripture.

GUIDELINES FOR THE CHURCH: Michael E. Haynes
I am going to discuss a simple lifestyle for the church from my experience as a member of a low-income urban black community, as a person who received welfare for many years and as one who today ministers among the poor, the black,

the Hispanic, the imprisoned and those who have just moved from poverty to the lower middle class.

Overview. In our Lord's parable of the talents, in his parable of the faithful servant and throughout the twelfth chapter of Luke, he warns his followers, "For unto whomsoever much is given, of them shall be much required; and to whom people have committed much, of them will they ask more" (adapted from Lk. 12:48 KJV). The statements of Paul in 1 Corinthians 16 indicate that the apostolic church recognized their responsibility to share their abundance with any part of the body of Christ that had need.

The spirit of the New Testament church (Acts 2:44-45; 4:34-35) should guide the church today. All the material resources and all the social influence which the Lord loans to his church are to be used for his glory, to extend his love and his grace to the world he came to save.

The church should obey the word of Jesus to the rich young ruler, "If thou wilt be perfect, go and sell that thou hast, and give to the poor, and thou shalt have treasure in heaven: and come and follow me" (Mt. 19:21 KJV). The church should declare certain corporate decisions to its members and to the world in order better to share its resources with the needy. The church should also be bold to urge the government, private foundations and wealthy individuals "to do justice, and to love kindness, and to walk humbly with your God" (Mic. 6:8).

Challenge to the black church. Since its inception the black church in America has been involved in the issues of human survival, justice and freedom. As it grows in influence and ability it must not lose its biblical perspective. Both ends of the black theological spectrum, left and right, need to heed the prophetic insight of the late James Weldon Johnson, who in the Black National Anthem (a misnomer) said:

God of our weary years, God of our silent tears,
Thou who has brought us safe thus far on our way,

Thou who hast by thy might, led us into the light
Keep us forever in thy path we pray.
Lest our feet stray from the places, our God, where we met
*   Thee,*
Lest our hearts drunk with the wine of the world, we forget
*   Thee!*

Although the black church does not even begin to have the land, buildings, endowments, stock portfolios and wealthy members that the white church does, it still has a mandate to share all the Lord loans it with the "society of need" both at home and abroad. In the United States and Canada and more so in the Caribbean and Africa, there are millions of our ethnic kinspeople, including brothers and sisters in Christ, who suffer inhuman poverty, oppression and persecution. We should consider sharing with them even the comparatively little which the landowners and wealth-controllers in America have allowed us to secure. The black church must share its resources, such as they are, with "whosoever will": white, black, red, yellow or brown. Whoever needs a cup of water, a crust of bread or the voice of an advocate.

Challenge to the white church. I have often found myself quoting a section of the Lord's prayer and applying it to white America and the white church establishment: "For thine is the kingdom, the power and the glory." Unfortunately, many people, including some evangelicals, act as if all the world's resources belong to them alone. Blacks, for reasons beyond their influence, control almost nothing in this country. They are still systematically exploited in their native land of Africa and wherever they are allowed or forced to live. Certainly there are other Third-World people who share a similar plight, and our concern is the same for them.

It is paradoxical and troubling that as soon as blacks seem to be gaining power politically, academically and economically, reverses set in. Whites are now returning to many American inner cities, while blacks are being moved out of core areas into restricted suburban communities as a result of urban renewal and the efforts of realtors, banks and other lending sources. Affirmative action and equal opportunity programs are being sabotaged across this nation. While the government spends billions of American dollars for Israeli-Egyptian peace it scuttles human services to minorities, the aged and the poor.

A study of any major North American missionary conference shows that the evangelical establishment still gives low priority to blacks and other needy minority people in America. It appears that the evangelical establishment still has a sense of *personal pride* and ownership in the wealth, influence and wisdom which the Lord God has loaned to it for his glory. As difficult, inconvenient and uncomfortable as it is to do, the evangelical establishment needs to generously and courageously and faithfully obey the biblical command to forsake selfishness and become true stewards of all that the Lord has temporarily placed in its trust.

Some practical guidelines. I submit the following passages of Scripture as guidelines for individual Christians and the church.

James 1:17: "Every good gift and every perfect gift is from above, and cometh down from the Father of lights, with whom is no variableness, neither shadow of turning" (KJV). We cannot brag about the resources we have as if we own them by our might, wisdom, goodness or industry.

Matthew 22:39: "Thou shalt love thy neighbour as thyself" (KJV). We are to have an attitude of consideration, concern and service to our fellow humans, our neighbors.

Matthew 5:44: "But I say unto you, Love your enemies" (KJV). We are to love even people whom we do not like, whom we feel alien toward, to whom we dare to feel superior.

Luke 6:30: "Give to every man that asketh of thee; and of him that taketh away thy goods ask them not again" (KJV). Jesus commands that those who have financial resources and possessions are to share with those who have less.

Bible-believing churches, preaching the Second Coming of Christ, should be more than willing to share significant portions of their endowments, investments and portfolios with poor Bible-believing congregations, with poor Christian young people seeking an education (especially in Christian ministries) and with human service agencies in underprivileged areas. Further, economically secure Christian institutions should try to make job opportunities and training programs available to the "have nots."

All Bible-believing Christians must be careful not to become modern-day Pharisees: self-righteous and superior before the lost and downtrodden of our society, acting as if we have an exclusive claim on God. We must recognize the brevity of life, the shallowness of material gain and our total dependence on and accountability to the Lord Jesus Christ before whom we must ultimately stand.

Perhaps the real question is: do we really believe God's Word?

LIVING WORD COMMUNITY—Philadelphia:
Ronald L. Klaus

In the late 1960s the leadership of the Living Word Community (then known as Philadelphia Gospel Temple) undertook an intensive look at their group. What were their strengths and weaknesses, their particular call? They found strengths in the areas of worship and teaching ministry, along with a sense of enthusiasm and of God's moving.

But several weaknesses became evident. First of all, genuine New Testament koinonia seemed rare. People were friendly to each other, but in the context of the large meetings that were typical for the church, deep personal sharing did not occur. Most people did not know many other people very well, let alone their needs and problems. As a result there was little practical ministry to one another.

A second need was lack of significant spiritual leadership. Although John Poole provided gifted overall leadership, few other men were affecting people spiritually in a profound way. The church structure seemed to militate against developing spiritual gifts on a large and widely distributed scale.

Those considerations led the church into a year of study and searching for direction. During that time a core of people was raised up who were committed to a radically different kind of church structure—one that would facilitate koinonia and permit spiritual leadership to emerge in a natural way. After that time of study, a crisis was precipitated and the church reorganized itself in a radically different way. All central activities such as Sunday school, women's groups and so on, were discontinued with the exception of one weekend worship service. In place of the disbanded activities, home meetings were established in different geographical areas, each with its own leader. Those leaders were specifically related to older, more mature leaders in accountable relationships. The home-meeting leaders were seen as "local pastors" and given genuine responsibility for the spiritual development of the people in their groups. They, in turn, were supported by elders who then became, in a sense, pastors of pastors.

That reorganization was controversial and many people left the church. Yet the home meetings were the beginning of a ministry in which personal needs and problems, both spiritual and practical, were addressed in specific ways. If someone was experiencing a difficulty or trial, he or she was offered the prayer support of people who really knew them. Counseling from more mature members was also available. Practical problems such as house repairs, moving, baby-sitting and help during illness, became concerns of the home meetings, and people began to learn to know and help one another. For many single people, the home meetings became a kind of loving family. For families, the meetings were a kind of "family of families" in which additional resources could be shared.

New church structure and new attitudes led the church into a period of explosive growth. From the start of four home meetings, the community grew in a few years to over fifty such groups. As people were added, the original congregation expanded until the building could no longer accommodate them. At that time a decision was made not to invest in buildings, but rather to split the congregation. Thus in 1972 a second congregation, in nearby Cherry Hill, New Jersey, was formed. By 1976 those congregations had grown to the point where they were both split again. The four resulting congregations became know as the Living Word Community which at its peak had more than a thousand committed members.

Parallel to numerical growth was the growth in the trained leaders of home meetings. Gifted men were able to disciple others in their groups into positions of leadership, and those persons, in turn, eventually led groups themselves. As a result, clusters of groups began to develop in various geographical areas, forming the nuclei of the various congregations. Through all of this, emphasis continued to be placed on the development of nurturing relationships. Since people were encouraged to find and develop any ministry to which God was calling them, the home meetings provided a natural outlet and context for such ministry. The emphasis of the elders shifted very much toward the development of leaders who would actually carry out the ministry of the fellowship. Thus the elders became "equippers" of the saints for the work of ministry (Eph. 4:12).

A serious crisis took place in 1976 when John Poole left the community. He had been used by the Lord to spearhead the changes, and his widely known public teaching ministry was an important asset of the community. At that time, one of the congregations elected to leave the community and has functioned independently along similar lines. The three others remained together, led by a group of elders. Perhaps the greatest test of the validity of such a church structure is whether the congregations continue to develop and grow without charismatic leadership.

Lately there has been a clearer recognition that community is not an end in itself but a means toward ministry and mission. As a result some of the groups have become more mission-oriented. Several groups now have a special outreach to women and students. Interest in the arts has increased. Christian artists are coming together and finding fellowship to support each other in their life callings.

As people have come to know each other through the home meetings, their personal lifestyles have begun to be affected. Many have changed their living situations to live more closely together. In some cases that has meant living under the same roof; in other cases people have moved to the same neighborhood. The Living Word Community thus has within it several different models of lifestyle. Extended households have invited single people to share in the family life of a married couple and their children. Some families share the same house. Quite a few single people have moved into apartments or houses together, often with a more mature couple living nearby. Some single people have been invited to share partially in the life of a particular family without actually living with them. They share some meals together, participate in some of the family activities and bear some responsibility for duties and chores. The Living Word Community has endeavored to tailor the kind of community life to the needs of its people.

A simpler lifestyle has often been a by-product. As people have gotten to know each other in depth, they have been able to share resources, easing their individual economic burdens and providing a better base from which to minister to the many needy people outside the community.

*Address: Living Word Community, 142 N. 17th St., Phila-
delphia, Pa. 19103*

SOJOURNERS FELLOWSHIP—Washington, D.C.:
Joe Roos

Sojourners Fellowship is a young and growing church located in inner-city Washington, D.C. Our beginnings can be
traced to the days of the *Post American* (predecessor to *Sojourners* magazine) in Chicago, Illinois, in the early 1970s.
From that beginning to the present, one of the central parts
of our vision of community has been the call to simple living.

Spiritually, we understand from the teachings of Jesus
that we are to live simply, unpreoccupied by physical needs,
living as though God was as concerned (or even more concerned) about our physical sustenance as he is about that of
the birds of the air and the lilies of the field. We are to seek
first the kingdom of God, assured that our physical needs
will not be neglected.

Jesus also taught that there was a fundamental contradic-
tion between the accumulation of wealth and possessions
and the worship of God. To be free from dependence on
"mammon" is to be free for dependence on God. We can fully
give ourselves to the kingdom only after we have broken our
idolatrous preoccupation with material acquisition.

It is as politically necessary for us to live simply as it is
spiritually necessary. Jesus displayed a profound identity
with the poor, an identity to which we as his followers are
also called. Scripture enjoins us to seek economic justice for
the poor as one way of identification. For Christians in the
United States, that scriptural imperative demands that we
break away from the patterns of overconsumption and waste
which characterize American lifestyle and play a significant
role in perpetuating poverty around the world and at home.

Simple living is therefore one of the pillars undergirding
the economic structure of our community's life. But an

equally important pillar is our understanding of what it means to be a church. We believe that to live in Christian community means to share our lives fully with one another, as though we were all brothers and sisters and part of the same family, as though the strength and vitality of the body of Christ were dependent in part on a deep sharing of who we each are: our growth and sin, our strength and weakness, our joy and pain, our anger and love. It includes the sharing of our gifts, vocation, ministry, relationships, marriage and singleness. In that sharing we are restored, encouraged, confronted and held accountable.

We also share our economic lives. We do not make economic decisions in isolation; they are made in a relationship of trust and accountability. Where we work; how much income is earned; how much is spent on rent, food, clothing, long-distance calls; where and how one goes on vacation; how much spending money one has and so on are all "submitted decisions," not strictly up to the individual.

We believe that the principle of economic sharing is foundational to the life and teaching of the New Testament church and is therefore binding on the church today. We do not believe, however, that any particular form is normative. The form of economic sharing becomes a function of the circumstances of a given church's life.

In addition to living simply and sharing our lives economically, we believe in the principle of lifestyle equality. That doesn't mean that everyone spends exactly the same amount of money and lives precisely the same way as everyone else. There is room for flexibility in need and interest. But it does mean that we all live at essentially the same level.

Simple living, economic sharing and equality of lifestyle are thus the principles underlying the economic framework of our life.

The economic structure of our community is separated into two independent entities. One governs the finances of our living situations, the other our ministries. The responsibility for financial oversight of the community is given to a group of five "administrators," who pay attention to the details of administering both entities, and a group of six "elders," who have final responsibility for oversight of the entire community.

In order to understand the economic structure of our living situation, it is helpful to know a little about our community structure in general. There are sixty core members in Sojourners Fellowship. Forty members live in four households and the remaining twenty live in smaller units. Each person belongs to one of five "small groups." It is in the small group that shared life and accountability occur most deeply; therefore, it is also in the small group that economic sharing and accountability are experienced most directly.

Each living unit has responsibility for determination of its own budget. The budget figures are based on need, not on income levels, and are compiled in accordance with the principles mentioned earlier. After the budget is shared with the small group, where it is discussed and any helpful changes are made, it is then reviewed by the administrators and elders. In that manner, all living needs of the community are determined in a way consistent with our commitment to simple living, economic sharing and equality of lifestyle.

The "common pot" seems for us to be the most efficient method of administering the finances of our living situations. All incomes (with a couple of exceptions for administrative reasons) are submitted to a central account. Funds then become disbursed according to need.

Whenever possible, we decentralize responsibility for the payment of living expenses into the hands of each living unit. That minimizes the administrative workload for the central account while maximizing the financial integrity and responsibility of each living unit. At the present time we decentralize rent, food, utilities, clothing, maintenance and personal spending money. Medical and transportation expenses are more effectively handled through the central account.

Some of the practical results are these: total monthly living expenses for a member average about $200; food runs $1.25 per person per day; each adult receives $15 spending money per month; clothing expenses are under $5 per person per month, except for children and those whose jobs necessitate somewhat higher amounts; used cars are purchased and assigned to small groups (not individuals) as needed.

Hospitalization insurance is carried only by those few who have coverage through their jobs. For the rest of the community, a cash reserve is used in the event of hospital stay. If the hospital expenses should exceed the cash reserve, we would pay the remainder in monthly installments and/or rely upon financial assistance from other churches with whom we are in relationship. We would assist them in similar emergencies.

The other financial entity governs our ministries, which include *Sojourners* magazine, peace ministries, a day-care center, food store, a program for neighborhood children and one to work to alleviate Washington's housing crisis. A non-profit organization, Peoples Christian Coalition, was established to administer the finances and activity of each of those ministries.

Each ministry's budget is submitted to the administrators and elders for approval. Subscriptions and contributions provide income for the magazine and peace ministries. Local contributions and small community industry (a typesetting business and a book service) generate income for the other ministries.

Because of our peace commitments we are also committed to war-tax resistance, both personally and institutionally. Most people in the community either have no income or receive subsistence salaries which are below the taxable level, thus incurring no war-tax liability. For those at taxable income levels: when insufficient tax has been withheld, there has been refusal to pay the rest; when sufficient tax is withheld by the employer, we are pursuing ways to reduce war-tax liability to zero. Our goal is that no member of Sojourners Fellowship will be paying war taxes. We pay also no telephone excise tax.

The Peoples Christian Coalition is required by law to withhold federal income taxes (including war taxes) from employees' salaries and submit them to the government. When one family's subsistence needs became higher than the taxable level, we found ourselves in a moral predicament. We resolved our dilemma by refusing to cooperate with the war-tax collection. Since January 1977 we have withheld but not submitted federal income taxes from that employee's wages. We cannot institutionally collect for the government the war taxes we will not pay personally.

Address: Sojourners Fellowship, 1309 L St. NW, Washington, D.C. 20005

NATIONAL PRESBYTERIAN CHURCH—Washington, D.C.: Colleen Evans and Virginia MacLaury

It is with a deep sense of humility that we of National Presbyterian Church respond to a request for a paper on simple lifestyles. Dating back to the late 1700s the predecessor congregations of National Presbyterian Church have built a church of strong tradition and heritage. To be a witness to our "Reformed faith" in our nation's capital—as well as a parish church—National Presbyterian Church dedicated a cathedrallike home in 1970, a building of great beauty but a facility which many would not describe as in keeping with "a simple lifestyle."

We tell you this to give you some idea of where we are coming from. Tradition is the soil in which we all germinate.

Some Christians choose to leave the soil of the established church and stimulate it to meet the challenge of a new day with its issues. Yes, at times tradition and heritage are obstacles to change, but they may also be the ballast that keeps a ship upright as powerful winds of a new era fill its sails and drive it forward to fresh destinations.

To change metaphors, because a church is a living thing, its branches can be pruned and trained to new shapes for a new day. Slow—yes, but that is what some of us feel called to do. We feel that the bush that has stood the storms of history, having been prophetically shaped by response to issues of yesteryear, is worth cultivating and pruning to meet today's challenges.

Thus we ask you to bear with us if our humble beginnings seem small in comparison with the great strides of other brothers and sisters in Christ. We believe that our struggles to balance the old and the new are typical of a great number of Christian churches today, and therefore we have agreed to share our pilgrimage with you.

Our most specific attempt to encourage our congregation to focus on lifestyles began in 1975 when a dedicated band of concerned people felt led to do something, however small, about alleviating world hunger. But what to do? A special collection? A fair? A rummage sale? All of those time-honored but tired methods seemed to miss the point. It was easy for our relatively well-to-do congregation simply to write another check. That would not make us examine our own lives and think of the true meaning of sacrificial giving.

After a period of studying world hunger and learning what others were doing, it was decided to develop a Hunger Covenant. People were urged to covenant with the Lord to sacrifice something that would simplify their lifestyle or eliminate a wasteful practice in order to accumulate funds for a Hunger Task Force. A dinner was given to dramatize the need, with members randomly receiving either an ample and delicious chicken dinner, a low-cost starchy meal or a single boiled potato. People analyzed their emotional reactions of resentment, self-pity, embarrassment and guilt as some ate luxuriously while others looked on hungrily.

The dinner was a huge success, but even so, only a small percentage of the congregation actually made the covenant. The monetary results were good enough, however, to encourage the dedicated few. During the first year about $6,000 was collected, with a surprise anonymous gift of another $5,000. Since then, the giving continues, with roughly $9,000 received for hunger as a result of life simplification this last year. The proceeds are divided about evenly between hunger missions abroad (a village in India) and those in the Washington area.

The things people chose to give up reflect their middle-class culture. Some saw it as an opportunity to discipline themselves in a battle against smoking. One woman gave up her daily glass of wine before dinner. Some began carrying bag lunches to work instead of consuming expensive and excessive restaurant fare. Others chose to serve a meatless dinner once a week (many families have a soup night), or to stop using fertilizer on their lawn, or to eliminate grain alcohol at their frequent dinners and parties. One person saves all her sales slips and gives a percentage tithe to the Hunger Task Force. One young man who lives in Bethesda and works on Capitol Hill rides his bike approximately twenty-five miles back and forth each day (weather permitting) to save gas and money. There are tables in the church to receive food every Sunday—some of that food goes to the hungry in the District of Columbia; some stays at the church for people off the street and for church members with needs. Each Sunday as we come to worship, the food is a reminder of the poor.

Radically changed lives? No. But hopefully our efforts are consciousness-raising. They are a first step along the way.

Our next efforts were directed toward developing an

Urban Ministry Team. Although half of our "hunger money" went to the poor of Washington, most of the people in our congregation had never set foot inside a real slum. It was suggested that people donate time and talent directly to serve the needy and in the process develop greater understanding. In cooperation with minority leaders engaged in such ministry, National Presbyterian people began to go into poor neighborhoods to clean, paint and repair run-down buildings.

On one day recently the folks from National Presbyterian arrived at one of the work sites with all the makings of a potluck dinner. Workers and ghetto dwellers gathered in the basement of a local church to fellowship together with song and laughter. There was a guitar solo and a chorus of "Amazing Grace." An old black woman sang her own song to a soul beat. An elderly blind man gave his heart to "What a Friend We Have in Jesus." It was a joyous, spontaneous, loving experience—a far cry from the typical Washington dinner party known by many of our members.

National Presbyterians go home from those experiences with a new sense of commitment and a hundred questions. What good does it do simply to paint and clean a little? How can we do more than apply band-aids? How can we help to overcome the depression—and oppression—that gets in the way of poor people's helping themselves? What are the roots of poverty? Are those root problems a spiritual matter? For them? For us?

And so we began our next consciousness-raising project: a seminar series devoted to grappling with those questions and many more. Entitled "The Wrestlers: Where the Rubber Meets the Road," National Presbyterians meet every Sunday between services to discuss the real meaning of Christian commitment. Among others, we have had guests from the Sojourners and from the Church of the Savior come to share their way of living out commitment, of simplifying lifestyles, of dealing with social problems within a biblical, Christian context. Out of that we hope will come greater lifestyle changes, greater commitment to action, a deep honest look at "Christianity and money."

Some people have already made significant changes. A middle-aged couple with grown children moved from an expensive suburban neighborhood to a modest city apartment to be closer to their areas of Christian mission. A couple in similar circumstances bought an apartment house on Capitol Hill and became intensely involved in the problems of the poor of that area. Several other families moved into one inner-city block to form a "community of ministry." Many others are honestly looking for ways to live and "model" Christian love in the community.

There are problems, of course. Some Hunger Covenant members reluctantly admit that they sometimes give the money but don't really make the sacrifice they had pledged. Urban Ministry participants worry about being naive when the slum dwellers show up for dinners but not for the work detail.

Those are small problems, however, easily overcome or resolved. By far the most difficult challenge lies not within the small band of those in sympathy with these efforts, but rather in the many who remain on the sidelines. In a congregation of eighteen hundred, some two hundred participate in our Hunger Covenant, and much the same group of people makes up the Urban Ministry corps. We have much work to do in reaching our National Presbyterian brothers and sisters with a convincing portrayal of the need to care and conserve. We are mightily interested in a group devoted to exploring lifestyles. We need your ideas and your inspiration. We ask your help as we seek to serve Christ and the world he loves.

Address: National Presbyterian Church, 4101 Nebraska Ave., NW, Washington, D.C. 20016

JUBILEE FELLOWSHIP OF GERMANTOWN—
Philadelphia: Arbutus B. Sider

Jubilee Fellowship is a house church whose members live and meet in the Germantown section of Philadelphia. We have twenty members, nineteen children and thirteen other adults who are either exploring membership or are friends who attend regularly. We come from a variety of church backgrounds: Baptist, Brethren in Christ, Lutheran, Mennonite, Presbyterian, Quaker and United Church of Christ. Most of us live within walking distance of each other. We have been meeting together for worship and other activities for five years.

We chose the name *Jubilee* as an ideal for which we would all like to strive. To us it suggests, on the one hand, joy, jubilation and praise. On the other hand, it points to a willingness to share with each other and the poor beyond our Fellowship—in the spirit of the year of Jubilee (Lev. 25). That is the spirit that Jesus seems to have referred to in his first sermon, announcing that he had been chosen to "proclaim the year of the Lord's favor" (Lk. 4:14-28 NIV).

The nine people who first became Jubilee Fellowship had not originally planned to become a church. We found in each other's fellowship the support we needed in the city for the Christian values we believed in; it also seemed an important base for communicating those values to our children.

For almost five years our worship services were held in our homes. About six months ago we admitted the inevitable. We just didn't have room for everybody anymore. Fifteen children in a one-family house for a shared meal too often resulted in bedlam. The atmosphere was almost too intimate for visitors (imagine being offered a two-foot square patch of rug to sit on for two hours and then being surrounded by a roomful of hugging strangers).

In looking for a larger space we were quite clear that we did not want to put a lot of money into an expensive structure.

Our investigation of a number of possibilities finally led us to a neighborhood recreation center, Happy Hollow, which we are free to use in exchange for minimal contributions to the needs of the recreation program.

Although the building leaves a lot to be desired, it meets our present needs and gives us an additional tie-in with our neighborhood. It channels money into human needs rather than into expensive architecture. But is an ugly, graffiti-covered building with unpredictable heating, poor acoustics and disappearing furniture the best sanctuary for the Lord? We know that the Lord is present in his people, not the building. We know that simplicity does not preclude beauty, and we know that worship is not a time to escape from the ugliness of the world around us. Rather, worship is a time to bring the needs of the world into the beauty of his holiness. We can remind ourselves of that by cheering up our walls with some new banners and murals depicting symbols of our faith together with life in the city. The Lord is present in his sanctuary, no matter how humble it may be.

Our worship style has as much variety as the people leading it. The richness of that variety arises from the many different denominations we represent. We have compiled our own songbooks, and usually use guitar accompaniment. Some of our most beautiful and simplest services have been ones designed for both children and adults.

Other aspects of our common life are a business meeting once or twice a month, a yearly retreat, workshops and gatherings for fun. The fellowship is divided into four sharing and discipling groups which meet weekly. In those groups we aim to help and support one another in living the Christian life. Biweekly workdays in the spring, summer and fall provide opportunities to help each other with minor house repairs.

We live in separate households and do not share a common purse, but we share with one another as there is need.

Members are asked to give seven and a half percent of their incomes to the fellowship for common projects and expenses, and are encouraged to give the rest of their tithes and offerings to projects they choose themselves. We stress simple lifestyle, including careful consideration of what we spend our money on, in view of the poverty and injustice in the world.

Various examples of how we have tried to practice our theory that we should "live simply so others may simply live" come to mind. In the context of our small groups we feel free to share our family budgets and ask for help in making financial decisions. There we also gain helpful input on our relationship with our children. We come to our small group for counsel and admonition if we face a decision requiring additional time commitments. Decisions related to time priorities are much more difficult for us than those related to money.

We also encourage each other to use public transportation when possible. Two families in the fellowship have no cars, so there is freedom to use each other's vehicles. There is a great deal of sharing of other things, from lawn mowers to hedge clippers to flour. We pass on clothes as our children outgrow them, help each other find the best thrift shops, fabric stores, garage sales, recycling centers and so on. We share information about free or inexpensive recreation. We support local food co-ops, and buy some food in bulk. More With Less is a favorite cookbook. We try to limit eating out and frequently get together for shared meals in our homes.

Extensively shared child care makes it possible for mothers in Jubilee to have the choice of pursuing interests outside the home. A personal concern for each other's children as we care for them can enrich rather than hinder their development. Raising children is one of the hardest things to talk about because of the various approaches, yet learning from each other has helped us all. In several of our families women

do part of the wage earning; in all families we regard it important for fathers as well as mothers to have significant responsibility for their children.

Choosing to live in a "deteriorating neighborhood" from
which whites were fleeing did two things. It made it possible
for us to buy houses at very low cost ($4,000-$15,000 for two-
and three-story structures), and it enabled us to help turn
around the downhill trend in the neighborhood. When we
moved in, every street in the area seemed to have one or two
boarded-up, abandoned houses on it. Several of ours were
like that, needing complete renovation. Some of that work
we did together as a fellowship.

Leadership of the fellowship is not the responsibility of
ordained clergy or elders, but is shared by all members of the
fellowship, each of us doing jobs in accordance with the gifts
God has given us. Our structure includes the following
teams: (1) Teams that relate to the internal life of the fellowship: worship, adult teaching, children's concerns, counseling, hospitality, finance and coordinating. Basic policy-mak-
ing is by consensus. (2) Teams that relate to the external life
of the fellowship: Liberty to the Captives (concerned with
human rights issues) and Discipleship Workshops (concerned with world hunger and justice issues). Both of those
teams include people not a part of Jubilee Fellowship.

One member of Jubilee, Dick Taylor, is employed part-
time by the fellowship to coordinate and explore communi-
ty-action projects. The decision to employ Dick was made
because we recognized we had run out of volunteer time, yet
believed it was an area of service that needed to be expanded
in order to balance our strong concern for national and international justice. Community projects include preparing and
serving hot lunches to elderly people on Fridays at a nearby
Episcopal Church, a food cupboard for needy neighborhood
people (the food is gathered by us and dispersed by the Sisters of the Good Shepherd) and a joint project of members of

the Fellowship and the Sisters to improve living conditions for elderly, retarded and mentally ill people living in a neighborhood hotel.

Other projects related to the fellowship are Jubilee Fund, Jubilee Crafts and *The Other Side* magazine. Members of the fellowship participate in Mobilization for Survival, Evangelicals for Social Action, various neighborhood and housing organizations, food and nursery cooperatives, Parents' Union (watchdogs over the public schools), an after-school Bible class for neighborhood children and a recreation program for retarded children. Several members have jobs outside the fellowship which are also concerned with sharing the whole gospel. They include work at a geriatric agency, public health nursing, a parachurch mission education organization, and high-school, college and seminary teaching.

If that array of church activity sounds anything but simple, the criticism is well taken. Having too much to do and not enough time to do it is the aspect of our life together that we struggle with more than any other. Some of us constantly feel a need to work at simplifying that part of our lives, to keep a healthy rhythm between the nurturing of the inward life and the activity of the outward, between structured work time and informal interaction with each other and our neighbors. What can be said on the other hand is that many of the commitments described above are regular jobs and not activities that must be fitted in after five or on weekends only. Also, much individual choice is expressed in how full one's life gets. We put greatest emphasis on the Tuesday evening small-group time together, then on the Sunday morning worship, then on participation in at least one Jubilee team. Beyond that a person can choose to participate or not, depending on the needs of the individual—and of course on his or her ability to say "No."

We have had to face other difficulties in our choice of community and church life. The fact that we come from diverse backgrounds adds tension, but our common commitment to the authority of Scripture and to Christ as Lord provides an anchoring center for our life together. Our consensus model of decision making is slow and sometimes delays progress for considerable time. We are unhappy about the fact that we are an isolated congregation unrelated to any denomination, yet our diverse backgrounds make it somewhat difficult to find a larger body to which to relate. We are, however, actively working at that problem and have made significant progress.

We are also not pleased with the fact that we are predominantly a white, middle-class group. We have not as yet been able to break through class, ethnic and educational barriers to become a truly multiracial, multiclass church. We pray that God will help us change that.

Address: Jubilee Fellowship of Germantown, 312 W. Logan St., Philadelphia, Pa. 19144

PATCHWORK CENTRAL—Evansville: Elaine M. Amerson

Some ten years after college and having lived in various settings around the world, my husband Phil and I were beginning to be very serious about bringing wholeness into our individual, professional and family lives. We had seen enough poverty, alienation and need in Latin America and in the U.S. to know that we could not continue to live as if the only limits to our lifestyle were those incurred by our salaries.

What did the Scriptures have to say about lifestyle? An honest search—with the question in mind, "How shall we live in relationship to our neighbor?"—began to reveal that God had much in store for us. God's concern for the poor, God's admonitions to stewardship and against excess and God's call for availability of ourselves and our resources on behalf of our sisters and brothers, all led us to begin making changes in our lifestyle as individuals and a family. Our theology began to be shaped more along the lines set forth by John V. Taylor in *Enough is Enough.*

Perhaps the most significant understanding on which we acted was the call to be in relationship with others as sojourners of the New Covenant—to live in community as an expression of our willingness to be available and our need to be supported in that journey. At that point in our pilgrimage we began thinking about founding a community. In community, "giving up things" is not the issue, but rather "all that is added" is significant. Intangibles like love, caring, value-sharing, dialog, dreaming together and acting with others far outweigh the value of the latest shoes and clothes, meat and so forth.

We now look back and are pleasantly surprised to find that the changes have been significant—and we continue to be a family that is changing. But it did not happen overnight. Our early efforts at simplifying our lives began with food: learning to cook and eat healthful, meatless meals and to cut down on sugar and sweets. (Some of those efforts are humorous to recall: lentil patties which looked like hamburgers were rejected by the children at first, but those days are now forgotten as they sometimes gobble two and ask for a third one).

Clothes were an issue that was not so difficult. I soon came to enjoy shopping with others at secondhand stores and rummage sales (it was more difficult when the rest of the country caught on to those stores as "old" clothes came back in style). Hand-me-downs that are cleaned and mended look and feel "like new."

Household items came into focus as we learned of ways to live with less. Secondhand store items and cast-off furnishings look at home in our 1890 house. Auctions in the Midwest are great family fun and yield functional and beautiful goodies for parents and children alike. For transportation, a commitment to use the bus when possible, ride bikes, walk and share car rides is important to us.

We are in process; we continue to learn and adapt. Sometimes it is not easy. The advertisements in newspapers, magazines, billboards and on radio and television all call on us to consume more. They even try to convince us that we are needy and should want more. We have made two choices that help us keep our perspective on being a people called to "eucharistic living": our economic situation and our life in community.

Moving to the Midwest. Our move to begin the dream of Patchwork Central in 1977 in Evansville, Indiana—an intentional Christian covenant community in an urban setting— was a choice that disallowed the automatic monthly paycheck from an institution and saw our income drop to one-third of what it had been. Issues like meat, fashion clothes and expensive entertainment are now moot points; one continues implementing simplified measures out of necessity (as is the case with the majority of the peoples of the world).

The community of brothers and sisters who are sharing their struggles and dreams, their material and personal resources, make the living joyful. Certain material goods do not have to be duplicated in each family: we have a community freezer, lawn mower, washers and dryers, garden tiller and so on. Sharing of cars, growing gardens, rehabilitating our old homes, baking and often eating together multiplies the fellowship and fun and diminishes the need for buying more and more as individual families.

We live in proximity and draw liberally from each other as we need encouragement, wisdom, comfort, advice, recreation and caring. Our children benefit as well. They are important, and much special emphasis is given to their concerns and interaction with the larger community. "Aunts" and "uncles" abound in the style of the almost-extinct extended family. Sharing child care is also a community gift.

Our ministry—to the neighborhood, the city and beyond— flows out of our shared life together. We study the Scriptures as we struggle to understand the direction our lives and our service should take. We celebrate the fact that we are a biblical people, living joyfully and intensely—with less. I no longer struggle with an answer to my daughter's question, "Mommy, are we rich or are we poor?" While I recognize her dilemma in trying to make sense of the media image of U.S. abundance in the midst of some obvious Evansville poverty, I have only one answer: We are rich. In this whole world we are among the wealthy—no matter how many more things you see that others have. And as God's people we have to share our education, expertise, goods and ourselves.

Our covenant relationship at Patchwork Central speaks to the commitment we share for our life together.

Covenant of Patchwork Central. As members of Patchwork Central, because we are committed to a daily living into the gospel, we accept certain disciplines of Christian community. Our covenants are stated specifically so that we may be clear as to the nature of our ministry, our commitment to care for the members of the community and in turn be cared for by them, and our common intention to live as people of the new order which is the kingdom of God. We affirm these disciplines as essential to our empowerment for ministry. While the community may call people to a ministry, it is our vision that empowered as covenant members we will not wait upon such a call but will be enabled to identify and freely offer our gifts of ministry.

We acknowledge that it is the nature of commitment not to be bound by or limited to these disciplines. We therefore will re-establish our covenants annually. We also acknowledge that each covenant will need to be shaped in terms of the uniqueness of every community member and that the fullness of time for most ministries will hardly fall in terms of an annual calendar. We therefore accept the place of negotiation among covenant members. Such rituals of negotiation should occur for the community both prior to the making of annual covenants and whenever the covenant of any one member seems inappropriate or detrimental to ministry. We affirm such covenant-making to be a signal of our common desire to live as the body of Christ in the world.

1. We commit ourselves to a specific time of personal prayer each day and to participation in community prayer time. We thereby recognize our responsibility for intercessory prayer for each member of the community and for his or her ministry. We will also agree to pray in specific terms for the needs in our neighborhood, city and for our sisters and brothers throughout the world.

2. We agree to participate in and periodically assume leadership for weekly eucharistic celebrations.

3. We commit ourselves to regular study, including the Scripture, so that our ministries may be enlightened. We also will participate in times of corporate study so that we might share our learnings and gain further insight into the ministries of others in our community. These times of corporate study will include participation in regularly scheduled community workshops, attendance at professional meetings, topical series specifically for community members, and at least two community retreats per year.

4. We will expect to see change both personally and in the lives of the persons with whom we work. We also covenant to work for change within the institutions in which we participate and in any institutions which block reconciliation and renewal (metanoia) given by Jesus the Liberator whereby oppression and death are overcome.

5. We will seek by our living and meeting together to educate the children of our community in the ever-opening ways of the gospel. It is our intention while spending time enjoying and affirming our children to encourage in them such virtues as justice, love, nonviolence, imagination and trust. We will also seek continually to relearn from them those qualities of childlikeness so valuable to the Christian.

6. Our commitment to the ministries of Patchwork Cen-

tral will be reflected in financial sharing. We agree to set aside at least five percent of our incomes for the ongoing ministry of the community. This reflects our belief that contemporary Christians should learn to "travel light" so that we may be made potent for ministry. We affirm a simple lifestyle which, while it does not deny our middle-class identities, nevertheless frees us for more meaningful forms of life together. We take seriously the continual struggle persons in our society have with money. We intend not to have our lives or ministries so shaped or distorted by financial stresses or success so as to discount our prior commitment to discipleship. We commit ourselves to continue to work on this common threat and through plain speaking among ourselves and the sharing of our resources to seek continually to give priority to seeing money used rightly, that is, for the furtherance of the kingdom.

7. I make the following specific identification of a ministry to which I will give myself during the next year:_____.

8. We commit ourselves to enhancing the common life of Patchwork Central including:

a. Involvement in workdays, shared meals, study and business meetings, times of common prayer and worship.

b. Working with other members of the community, I agree to find ways to create with my own hands products which may be income producing. The first of these will be_____.

c. Working with other members of the community, I will assist in creating symbols of our common life. The first of these will be _____.

9. The seasons of Kingdomtide and Advent will be given to the preparation of persons as new covenant members. A catechism on the covenant will be taught and the community at large will support this introduction to our common life by remembering and imagining the gifts of Immanuel for Patchwork Central. I commit myself to the sharing in this concern.

10. We recognize that some members of the covenant will be called to move to places beyond this community. At that point I agree to prepare the community for a departure by participating in a ritual of leave-taking.

Address: Patchwork Central, 431 Washington Ave., Evansville, Ind. 47713

LASALLE STREET CHURCH—Chicago: John L. Petersen

LaSalle Street Church is a diverse church. Because our congregation comes from all social and economic backgrounds, the journey toward simplicity takes many different paths for different people.

LaSalle is a bridge community that mixes incomes and lifestyles and makes a point of accepting people where they are and trying to help them toward where they should be. Our church is active in a variety of social programs which include things like housing, youth work, tutoring, counseling centers, senior citizens and a legal aid clinic.

Because of all the participation in social areas, many, if not most, of the major social issues of the day have been formally confronted through our church programs. It is likely that because of that most of the people at LaSalle Street Church are more sensitive than usual to such issues. Our church has a strong social action committee that pushes hard on world concerns through presentations and a social action newsletter.

In a number of sermons, our minister, Dr. William Leslie, has strongly advocated the concept of a graduated tithe. Based on the income tax model, the idea is that the more you make, the greater percentage you give—instead of increasing your lifestyle in direct proportion to increased income from promotions and raises. Our members are encouraged to take an increment of the increased income and add it to their tithe.

The reactions of our people to the issues of simple lifestyle go all the way from some who suggest that, regardless of how much an employer wants to pay, a responsible person should refuse to take any amount of money above a certain limit, to those on the upper-income side of the spectrum who simplify their lifestyle by buying smaller cars and taking less expensive vacations. We have found that all of our people have areas of extravagance, even those who advocate acutely simple lifestyles.

In addition to buying smaller cars and taking less costly vacations, a number of identifiable things have been "cut out" by our members in pursuing a simpler life. A number of families have sold their cars and now travel almost exclusively by public transportation. Large numbers have changed their eating habits in light of the world hunger situation. Quite a few of our families don't eat red meat, and some have cut out a great many of the foods that are conventionally eaten in our society. Some groups within the church choose not to spend money on new clothing.

Differing economic situations and differing commitments to lifestyle simplification have caused some amount of tension. Some of those more "radical" in their commitment to simplification and who have lived rather simply for most of their lives sometimes find it hard to relate to those who have worked very hard to get to where they are at the present time and for whom a drastic scaling down of lifestyle is not an option under consideration.

Our pastor voices his personal concern that lifestyle can become a new legalism in our very materialistic society by which spirituality is judged. He insists that the issue of lifestyle must be raised, but that it must not become legalistic. The job of the church is to be a bridge community between persons who have mixed incomes and lifestyles. Those with resources must be encouraged to be good stewards and to contribute in practical ways to the kingdom of God and society at large. They must also be encouraged and educated in their general sensitivity to those without money. A downward economic journey is generally accomplished in a series of steps. On the other hand, those without resources also need to learn to become accepting of those in higher income levels. The key word in our approach to this issue is *moderation.*

Lifestyle changes effected by the church among members came from raising the issue in three different ways: preaching, educational programs and cross-cultural contacts. Some sermons have focused on the issue as the main theme and in others it has been an underlying theme. We have regular programs, many of them sponsored by the Social Action Committee, that are primarily educational and centered around a major social issue. Many of our people also take part in the church's social ministries, and so are regularly exposed to those with far fewer resources than their own. In such ways the church communicates to the membership their need to simplify their personal lifestyles.

Address: LaSalle Street Church, 1136 N. LaSalle St., Chicago, Ill. 60610

TWELFTH BAPTIST CHURCH—Boston: Michael E. Haynes
In attempting to present the Twelfth Baptist Church of Boston as a model of a simple lifestyle, I am somewhat at a disadvantage—or more accurately, I feel in a dilemma. Black churches, by and large, like black people in this country, have *always* practiced the simple lifestyle. We have been too limited in opportunity to do otherwise.

Twelfth Baptist Church was founded in 1805 as the First Independent African Baptist Church of Beacon Hill, Boston. It came into being as the direct result of slavery, racial discrimination and oppression of black people in the United States. The first building was made with bricks formed with the hands of newly freed slaves and their children. The church's history is rich and exciting.

Two interrelated purposes have been woven into the fabric of 174 years of life for our still predominantly black congregation. The first is the saving gospel of Jesus Christ to bring humankind to eternal salvation. The second is the here-and-now liberation of blacks and other oppressed people by the mandate of God's Word.

Lavish, plush, cathedral-type churches, built from the ground up, have been comparatively rare in black American society. Many of the so-called large-structured black churches in the nation were purchased at exorbitant, exploitative costs from nonblack, often dying congregations. For the most part, the classic, so-called storefront church has been an understandable phenomenon of the black church in urban America.

The apostle Paul taught us in his sermon on Mars Hill that "God that made the world and all things therein... dwelleth not in temples made with hands" (Acts 17:24 KJV). Twelfth Baptist Church is presently housed in a "hand-me-down" building, which we have sought only to make bright, clean, functional and an honor to the service of our Lord Jesus Christ. We could have voted to "owe our soul to the company store" (for example, First National Bank) and tie up an economically limited congregation with a long mortgage. Rather, recognizing that the median income of our membership was limited, that large numbers were in unstable income situations, and that vital segments of our church family were recipients of public assistance, it was clear that a simple lifestyle had to guide our renovation plans and all we sought to do.

Of a ministerial team of four men and one woman, each of us has been led to become a member of the apostle Paul's "fraternity of tentmakers." Each team member has another occupation or source of income. That takes a financial burden off Twelfth Baptist Church and enables us to tithe and give more back into the fellowship. Thus more money is re-

leased to the witness of the gospel and to programs that help
raise the quality of life of those we are commissioned to
serve.

Coupled with ongoing efforts to conserve energy and
supplies, we are slowly moving toward a better stewardship
of the resources which our Lord has loaned to us.

*Address: Twelfth Baptist Church, 160 Warren St., Rox-
bury, Mass. 02219*

REBA PLACE FELLOWSHIP—Evanston: Virgil Vogt

At Reba Place Fellowship we began simplifying our lifestyle
because we were inspired by Jesus and his powerful teachings on the subject. It seemed clear, as we studied the New
Testament, that a fundamental change in the way we approach economic matters is an indispensable part of the gospel. To call people away from the idolatry of materialism is
thus a part of our evangelistic message. To teach people a
"kingdom approach" to finances has been an important and
blessed part of our congregational experience over the past
twenty-one years. That approach has found expression in a
complete sharing of all economic resources within the congregation, assets as well as income. About one hundred fifty-
five adults and their ninety children are currently participating in that pattern of congregational sharing at Reba Place.
We are also linked with several other communities that share
a similar approach.

The initial step that Jesus envisioned in his call to discipleship was renunciation of all we have. Hence we try to
call one another to an inner experience of "letting go" as part
of the conversion or church membership process. Expressing that by actually selling all and giving it away, or by turning one's resources over to the common treasury, helps to
make it a real experience.

After the initial step of renunciation and commitment, our
individual stewardship of economic matters is explicitly

under the authority of the church. We openly consult with others about our economic decisions and receive the counsel and support of the brotherhood in seeking to incorporate kingdom values in our lifestyle. A structure of small groups, elders and large congregational meetings is important to that process. Sharing our decisions with others helps to cut through the rationalization of self-interest which is so prevalent in the area of economics.

All resources are then put into a common fund. Individuals and families receive monthly allowances for food, clothing and personal incidentals. Other expenses—housing, transportation, medical and educational costs—are met directly from the common fund. Special needs not otherwise covered are handled on an individual basis. The funds of the community are also used in various forms of ministry and outreach.

That pattern of congregational sharing brings equality among the members, makes it possible to help those who are less resourceful and enables us to encourage one another in a simpler lifestyle.

Specific features of our financial sharing include the following:

1. The monthly food, clothing and personal allowance is approximately what we would get if on Cook County welfare. In a family of four, the two adults each receive $49 for food and $23 for personal allowance, including clothing.

2. Housing is corporately owned by a not-for-profit corporation and is managed and repaired by community members. That enables us to reap the benefits of volunteer labor, efficient management and some offsetting of inflationary costs. We are also able to establish common guidelines for efficiency, such as winter thermostat settings of 65° during the day and 55° at night. We decided a number of years ago to forego the use of summer air conditioning. A two-bedroom house in our neighborhood now rents for $280 to $350. Our

average housing cost is about $117 per person, including mortgages, repairs, utilities and telephone.

3. Cars are shared. That enables us to get along with thirty-two vehicles for 245 people. We are also able to use various vehicles to fit a variety of purposes, smaller or larger cars as needed, older cars around town, newer cars for longer trips. A few of each type serve the whole community. We usually drive our older cars until they are ready for the junk-yard. Current operating costs, including purchase, upkeep and repairs, are about fourteen cents per mile. We also encourage people to walk, ride bikes and take public transportation.

4. A small food co-op does corporate buying in those stores in which it is still possible to do better than the large chain stores.

5. The community operates an exchange "store" in which clothing and furniture that are no longer needed can be shared with others. Such items are available free. We also utilize thrift stores in the area for purchase of clothing. We frequently find our needs met in a most surprising manner, which to us is a sign of God's providential care.

6. We do not accumulate for future needs. We believe that God's supply of our needs is so definitely promised that we are free to invest all that we have in the present—for ourselves and others.

7. We seek to be content with what we have and to live without indebtedness. Purchasing real estate with mortgages is a specific exception.

8. We have felt called to turn away from insurance as a method of facing unknown future needs, believing that God's providential care and the sharing among Christians will be sufficient. That includes automobile insurance. We do carry a few insurance policies where it is required of us by others (for example, on buildings that have mortgages).

9. We try to encourage healthy living, we pray for the sick,

and we use medical clinics when we need medical care. Total medical and dental costs are currently about eighteen dollars per month per person.

10. We encourage modest vacations and recreational travel.

11. The average total cost of living at the present time is about $240 per adult and $210 per child, monthly.

12. About thirty percent of the wage earners contribute over fifty percent of their earnings to the work of the church (that is, their wages exceeded their own cost of living by that amount). An additional twenty percent contribute at least thirty percent of their earnings.

13. A rather extensive local ministry is supported by the community, including six to eight persons in full-time pastoral ministries. Needy persons have come to the community for various kinds of assistance.

14. In addition to local ministry (that is, personal support and local church) the community is moving toward a goal of contributing ten percent of gross income to needs beyond the church.

There are, of course, many joys and freedoms of communal living. We have had the joy of being able to get our priorities straight (to seek first the kingdom), putting human values ahead of economic values, letting finances be secondary in decisions that need to be made. Total sharing of finances builds a strong sense of community. Needy persons can receive subsidy without much fuss and without reinforcing a sense of inferiority. Their needs are evaluated and met on a par with others.

There is also security. Without having much, the community operates with little worry about finances. People know that their needs will be met, and they have given up on the drive to accumulate more and more. The sharing has functioned with a minimum of personal hassle, jealousies and resentments. People are freer to express their needs and also to borrow and lend freely.

Having a whole group trying to live a simple lifestyle makes it fun. We can laugh at ourselves and share good ideas; pressure to "keep up with the Joneses" is minimized. Art, music, dance and drama are very much alive in our midst.

Finally, I want to share some of our problems. First is ourselves. People trying to live closely and share fully with one another inevitably tangle with each other. We each bring our hurts and our ambitions which conflict with those of others. Having spiritual resources to solve problems and to live in Christlike love with one another is important.

Second, the effectiveness of the structure and the faithfulness of God in meeting our needs can lead to complacency. Sometimes people are not as careful with community property or community money as they would be if they were holding it individually. That has not been a large problem, but one we need to keep working on.

Third, there is still some economic anxiety and preoccupation. You can get as possessive or as anxious over the little that you have as others do over much. We need to keep teaching and encouraging a Spirit-filled approach to human experience.

Last, we are weak in working out our relationship to the very poor elsewhere in the world. We have taken some steps in generous sharing with others in other places, but that needs further development.

Address: Reba Place Fellowship, 727 Reba Place, Evanston, Ill. 60202

STRUGGLING FREE IN PROFESSIONAL LIFE: THREE TESTIMONIES

6

Howard Dahl, David Pullen and Dennis Wood participated in a panel discussion on professional concerns and how they relate to simple living. Each man first tells of his life and conversion and his personal pilgrimage of faith. These testimonies are followed by a question from the floor which was directed to the panel members.

HOWARD DAHL:
When I was growing up in rural North Dakota, the closest town of 5,000 people was sixty miles away. A "cross-cultural experience" meant meeting someone of German descent. That thoroughly Scandinavian town, was, you might say, a bit isolated. Because my grandfather didn't like the way his farm machinery worked, he started tinkering with

new farm machinery designs. About 1947 he decided he wanted to form a company. He went to a number of different towns and they said, "We don't want another blacksmith shop," so he ended up building a small company in a town of 150 people. That company, which our family no longer owns, now employs about 1,500 people in that small town. My father went on to develop a tractor company that now makes very large tractors of up to 450 horsepower. They make tractors under their own brand name, as well as all the large tractors for Ford and International Harvester.

When I went to college, I got caught up in the usual things. I was going to become an attorney and spend the rest of my life acquiring things and working with my family. But several things happened in college. I was active in sports, fraternity life, and then around the end of my freshman year some people came into our fraternity and talked about Christ. I can honestly say I had never heard anything like Billy Graham on TV. I'd never heard in my whole life that you were to have a personal relationship with Christ. What those people were saying was so overwhelming that I spent the next two weeks talking to them every day asking questions, and I made a kind of commitment to Christ at that time.

That was about 1968 and I was rooming with a guy whose father was a commander of the Marines in Vietnam. We did a lot of talking about what was going on there, and he became very involved in the counterculture.

Between my relationship to Christ, which was growing, and the activity on campus, a real change was taking place in my life. I wasn't quite sure where it was taking me, but my desires were gradually changing. I was planning to go into Naval flight training, but all of a sudden I started to realize all that that entailed. About midway through my junior year I was out at Aspen skiing, which my best friends and I did a couple of times every year. One day, skiing down the slopes I just said, "If this is the ultimate, if this is what life is all about, there's something that's sure empty inside me." I left my friends, went into Denver, and contacted some people I knew who were committed Christians. They laid some heavy things on me, and I might say that I really committed my life to Christ at that point.

I felt I needed to go into full-time Christian work. I had been active with Campus Crusade my senior year. So I went to work full-time on their staff at the University of Georgia and then for three years at the University of Florida. I met my wife in Georgia.

During the summer of my last year in Florida we had the opportunity to work with my dad's company in Hungary, where they were setting up a factory. I had not been exposed to the needs of the world in a very thorough way, but spending that summer in Hungary and talking with Hungarians opened my eyes to how wealthy we were. I had never seen the contrast before—and Hungary is certainly not a Third-World country. Since then I've been in Latin America and have seen the greater contrast there. But in Hungary I knew that my life was going to be taking another direction.

We went back to Florida where I did a year's graduate work in philosophy, and then went to seminary for two years. While in seminary I worked for a year at International Harvester's marketing research department. Three days after I got there I was assigned to do a feasibility study on a mission organization that was asking for a grant. As a result, I worked with that group for the next year and a half and my life was irrevocably changed. While I was at Harvester, I also worked on a United Nations study calling attention to the need for simple, low-cost tractors. It was a 200-page study saying there was going to be a need for hundreds of thousands of simple, easy-to-service tractors. I kept saying, "Somebody should do something, somebody should work on this," and I talked to everybody in Harvester that I could. I wrote memos to all sorts of people and found out that they weren't going to work on it because of the risk (I've written a paper about that elsewhere). I went to my dad's company, but their *smallest* tractor is 250 horsepower, and I could see that it didn't fit in very well with the program either.

To sum it up, my wife and I moved back to Fargo, North Dakota, two years ago and since then we've been working on what we consider a simple, easy-to-operate farm tractor. There's no steering wheel and no foot controls; a lot of thinking has gone into it. Two universities are doing testing on it, working with the United Nations in Africa. We're going to be very cautious before we introduce it in a large way. We've recently bought a small factory in Fargo that is ideally suited for the manufacture of tractors. We've got about 70 employees and right now we're doing custom metal fabricating.

Ann and I have wrestled a great deal with what is the right style of life for us because everything we grew up with is so different from the reality of the developing nations. We have received far more than we need to live on. In light of this, what does it mean to live responsibly? I spent more money in college than Ann and I have spent in our first four years of marriage, and I must say that I never started enjoying life at all until I started to live a lot more simply. I now have a great appreciation for even the littlest things, and I never had that before.

In what way am I to be my brother's keeper? That and other questions are not easy to answer, and we are just beginning to wrestle with them. In the midst of this search we have had a greater sense than ever of God's concern for the needy everywhere—those who are needy because they have too little and those who are needy because they have too much.

DAVID PULLEN:
I grew up in a Christian family in Paterson, New Jersey, and that is probably the greatest blessing God has given me. It was a poor family. Both of my parents were poor. My mother had

been orphaned when she was quite young. My father's father had died when he was seven, so his mother had raised him and the three other children in his family. We were struggling.

The area I grew up in was predominantly black. I was thinking about what Bill Pannell said the other day, about what it's like to live in the ghetto—that's what we had. But, unlike most of the blacks, I was able to get out. My parents had that option. They went deeply in debt but they got out. That itself is a drastic difference.

One thing that was very meaningful to me this summer was going back to Paterson and seeing what I really had been saved from. I may have lived there, but in one sense I didn't have to partake of the dead-end character of that situation in the same way that the blacks and Puerto Ricans and others who lived there with us did. My mother was a high-school dropout; my father was a college graduate. They emphasized knowing the Lord and Christian values. That enabled me to have certain values and led to my going on for an education. I went to Houghton College. I got into law school and then got drafted out of it, which was an upheaval in my life. Then I came back and finished law school in 1975.

I didn't know exactly what the Lord had for me, but he led, through a couple of strange turns, back to the Houghton area. I am presently working in a partnership in law with a man who, to the best of my knowledge, is not a Christian. He is a godly man, a God-fearing man, and a man of integrity. I have benefited from knowing him. It has been a good experience for me.

Probably one of the most critical events in my life was my marriage to a woman who had interests in becoming a missionary. My wife's interests coincided with some of the things I was beginning to feel and wrestle with. I started out as a person very deeply in debt, which, in a sense, I still am— paying off my education loans. But even with the debts and the limited possessions I had, the future before me was, in a sense, unlimited. As I looked at those around me—we live in Allegheny County—I realized we live in the poorest county in New York State, per capita. I believe it has the highest level of welfare recipients in the state. I've heard that it is one of the poorest counties in the country. In that county there are thirty attorneys. But for the poor, who are almost a third of the population, there is only Southern Tier Legal Services with one attorney three half-days a week. The other two-thirds of the people have the thirty attorneys in the private bar. You can figure out the percentages of what that means per capita for the poor as far as legal aid is concerned.

Legal help goes where the money is; you develop the areas of expertise that make a return. So in areas such as Social Security, SSI, welfare services—no lawyers have any expertise in that except the legal aid people, because there's no money in it. Those people do not have retainers that they can pay to the attorneys. So when a private attorney gets called on a case, even if he's disposed to take the case, he has to turn it down because he has no expertise in the issues that concern the poor. The welfare regulations, for instance, are an exercise in insanity. Coupled with that is the way the system works—seventy percent of the decisions that are appealed as having been made improperly are overturned. So the poor are wrestling with a system which is, either by design or just by the sheer complexity of it, functioning improperly most of the time.

As I became aware of this, I just couldn't turn my back on it. My partner is now seventy-three years old and will probably be retiring this summer. I'm now twenty-nine years old. That means that by the time I'm thirty I will own a prosperous practice. It is in the northern end of the county—it is *the* practice to have. My income has doubled each year I've been there. Faced with that, my wife and I have had to confront questions of how we would dispose of that wealth. What the Lord has impressed on me is, in a sense, that the wealth itself is a cop-out, and what he is calling me to now is to consider a clinic. I would support myself through the practice I have, and once we have enough to live on, to meet our basic needs, then the rest of the time would go into the clinic for meeting the needs of the indigent.

The idea of living simply to put time into a legal service clinic runs counter to the traditional lifestyle of most of the people around us. Along with that there are also our own personal questions. We have had to wrestle with retirement. I don't have an employer taking pension payments and savings out of my paycheck. So what will I do about retirement? The passage in 2 Corinthians where Paul speaks about giving has come up a couple of times. There are *present* needs of people, and yet retirement is a future need. As a result I've had to say, "I'm going to have to trust God for the future. Right now what he has blessed me with is still his—he's just given it to me to be a steward." So the property we have received, the wealth, we have basically passed on. We have no retirement plan.

We have also struggled with the question of medical insurance, and we've put aside what medical insurance would have cost. We have set up a savings account (the only one we have) for our medical needs and the needs of people the Lord brings to us. That overcame some of the problems I saw inherent in the insurance industry with its profit maximization goal: they're in a sense betting you're going to stay healthy and you're betting you're going to get sick. I'm going to have to trust the Lord for that too. It will cover moderate expenses. When Seth, our son, was born, it covered that—but it's not going to cover a prolonged illness.

The other thing we've had to wrestle with is ownership of property. At the present time, we couldn't possibly live as cheaply owning a place as we can in a home that the Lord provided. John and Carolyn Miller were missionaries in Vietnam. When they came back the Lord provided money, so they bought a place to be a homestead for their family when they come home on furloughs. When they're in the field their home is vacant. We had been married just a short time when their fully furnished house became available. For the present time, that's our home. We've struggled with that—we're not building any equity in it—but it is providing a home for now, and the future is in the Lord's hands.

The big test is going to come if we have some emergencies which require us to go back to a more income-producing setup than the ministry we feel the Lord calling us to now. When I wrestle with that, I get scared. Family and friends have asked the question, "If you get sick, and you have high medical expenses, what are we supposed to do? You say you're trusting the Lord, but how will we be expected to respond?" They've used that as a club, in a sense, against us. That's a serious question. I don't know what to do with it. Those friends and family members are going to have to follow the Lord and seek him as to what their wealth should be used for, as we're doing now.

At this point in our lives I feel my wife and I are just experimenting, putting our toes in the water. We haven't been tested and tried to see how long our convictions will last. I don't know whether I've got the faith in the Lord that will stand the tests that I believe he'll bring. Dennis Wood mentioned growing through suffering. I use the phrase *being conformed to the image of Christ*. I haven't liked a lot of what the Lord has done in my life as he's done it. But as I look back it's been good, and I'm glad. But we're just beginning. I'd appreciate your prayers and advice and models.

DENNIS WOOD:
I want to begin by saying that as Jayne and I have worked with lifestyle, we've defined it somewhat more broadly than

we've discussed it at the Consultation, which is to say it's all of who we are. We look at time, energy, effort, our objectives, our priorities and our material wealth as being our lifestyle. That's using the term in a much broader sense.

I grew up on a farm in Oregon—seven children, not very much money, but we didn't lack very much either. At the same time, there wasn't a lot of opportunity. Most people didn't leave rural Oregon, or leave it for much better. As I was growing up, things that a non-Christian would look at and say were "lucky breaks" occurred in my life, and I began to know how to exploit those. It went on through high school and through college. I was State President of the Future Farmers of America, won national public-speaking contests and things like that. Some of it came from my father's saying, "If I had it to do again, I'd be a lawyer." Some came from my own ambition saying, "What's really important to me is to hold power."

Money didn't bother me very much, but to move, to be successful, to be liked, to be seen as being somebody, was important to me. It was the only way to get from where I grew up in rural Oregon to where someone else would recognize me and say, "That guy's all right."

That kind of ambition, that kind of motive or drive, was very significant for me. It carried me through undergraduate school and scholarships and all the events where you have to succeed by competing, by being better than somebody else, by knocking somebody else off the track—doing it in a nice way—but still making sure somehow that you are there ahead of everybody else. I saw graduate school, too, as a further means to success, and moving beyond that to law school primarily because I was very interested in politics.

It took me a long time—through law school and into the beginning job—to see in my own life that my driving ambition, particularly political ambition, was simply running my life. That realization came through a lot of community, a lot of Christian support, and brought me to the point where I could say before God (and eventually before my church community), "I set this aside; it's no longer important for me to be active in the political world or to be successful on those terms." Once I was able to say that before God, my life began to straighten out a little. It began to simplify my lifestyle *a lot*.

I moved through three years of consulting at Arthur D. Little in Boston. I went to Harvard Law School for a Juris Doctor degree and got a Ph.D. in International Agricultural Development. I had some good credentials to use in consulting and I liked it. Out of that context God suddenly picked me up—it wasn't *so* sudden as you look back on it—and put me right back into politics, in the government, in Washington, in the White House in the middle of the Nixon era, where I didn't want to go (having a McGovern sticker on my truck). But I went out of a much different sense—again still struggling, still striving, still ambitious, as much there for myself as I was there for God—not wanting to go yet feeling I must. We had been in a Christian community praying that God would raise up Christian men in the White House when I was suddenly asked to go there as a technical person for three months. As I flew to Washington I said to God, "That is *not* what I had in mind!"

I stayed and worked in the White House and the State Department for four years. As I saw the developing world and worked in it, as I began to understand how much I had in talent, education, material wealth and well-being, in contrast with all the other people in the world, I began to recognize that my life was *not* integrated. My objectives and desires were simply not aligned with what I was beginning to see around me in the world.

I found very little help for that in my fundamentalist Christian background and the churches I was in. I struggled mightily to integrate my Christian beliefs with what I was finding all about me. When I came to Washington, I found Church of the Saviour to be a helpful place to integrate who I was as a Christian with an "outward journey" in our world of pain and suffering and need. In that institution and through the many people who cared for me with a high level of commitment to discipline, I began to grow as a person. I questioned who I was and what my directions, objectives, priorities and standards were and how I could get them in order. I met and married Jayne at the Church of the Saviour and began then to think actively about how to integrate these two important parts of me: who I was as a Christian and what that meant with respect to the Third and Fourth Worlds.

Life was awfully busy and although we were on a track that asked, "Could we change our lifestyle?" somehow we couldn't. Jayne and I both worked at high-income jobs that were relatively important in the Washington sphere. Our jobs had obligations: sixteen-hour days sometimes, maybe more. They had social obligations. They had values attached to them and their institutions. Frankly, as much as we tried, we couldn't change very much. When we needed money, we had it. We had to go to cocktail parties and we usually didn't have time for the people who were important to us and the things we really wanted to be about.

In the mission group context of the Church of the Saviour, both Jayne and I came to the same conclusions. God was calling us to work with and on behalf of low-income people, and to get out of what we called "the rat race" and "upward mobility game." Doing that was easier when I lost my job (it was a matter of politics when the administration changed). That was God working in my life. I might have made the change eventually, but I made it much more suddenly because I had to. I was ready for it; it didn't come precipitously and it wasn't an anguished time. But I don't think I would have had at that time the courage simply to quit.

But that change *did* come, and what we developed as a result of my consulting experience with Arthur D. Little, my experience at policy levels in the government, and my own agricultural background was Devres, a small consulting firm to work on Third and Fourth World issues. It's in the marketplace. We largely work for USAID, the World Bank, the Food and Agricultural Organization, the United Nations Industrial Organization—people who, by and large, are in sympathy with our goal of working with and for low-income people, even with all the problems and difficulties of those agencies.

Beginning Devres has been a grave struggle for us. It's also been interesting, exciting—and clearly God's call in our lives. We've done good work on behalf of the poor in developing countries, and we have good people who do it. At the same time it has not proceeded the way I thought it would. Devres has not grown fast, and we've made very little money. At the same time we feel it's exactly right for us and where we're supposed to be. So we've grown in that sense.

We feel we're going to grow a little more soon. In the past we have had an income in our family which Jayne has been supplying. She's continued to work, but not in the consulting firm. The first year we were in business we did about $30,000, the second year about $68,000 and this year we'll do more, but that's paying for five people, office space, typewriters and everything else, so there hasn't been much to take home. It's that simple.

Now we're about to have a baby, and Jayne will earn less money, if any. We're simply having to say, "Lord, you know where we are and you know what we're about and you know we're supposed to be here." We find it very frightening, because we like security, and we like that sense of having—knowing—where our security is, knowing where our money's coming from, knowing how things are going to be for us. So the struggles we're facing now are financial—security, what is it in? We're at a point where we're vulnerable, *really* vulnerable for the first time in our lives since we were children, practically. And we're really saying, "Lord, are you going to be there? Is this really right?" We're excited about what we're learning and will learn in the future.

A QUESTION ABOUT INSURANCE

Charles Day: An issue that I'd like to say a word about is the subject of insurance. I think that one cooperative living arrangement said they carried no life insurance, no medical insurance, and as little automobile insurance as state law would allow. Other papers have made similar references.

That causes me a great deal of concern, because choices are being made by people here in this room to cancel insurance policies (and I'm not in the insurance business!). I think it is necessary to reflect on our responsibility to others, for example, if you have a car and you hit somebody and you disable them, somebody's got to be responsible for rehabilitating that person. I don't think it's fair just to say, "The Lord will take care of that somehow." If somebody in your group gets ill, or has some accident, and the need for rehabilitation comes up, there should be some provision. Perhaps the Lord also invented insurance companies to help make that kind of thing possible. My own opinion would be that one *could* look around and find various kinds of mutual companies or church-sponsored groups, or perhaps slightly untraditional ways of insuring, at least for medical needs and automobile insurance. I wonder if some of the members of the panel might have some reaction to that. Have you all seen fit to reduce insurance or do you still carry insurance? What is your recommendation?

Dennis Wood: I can comment from our experience on insurance. If you look at the configuration Jayne and I find ourselves in now, our family life and our assets are mixed up with our company. Our company does government contracting of all kinds, so our insurance must be sufficient on a company basis. For me, since I'm key in the company, it is sufficient that, if I die, Jayne can "get out whole," that is, at that point where all the debt structure (it's a substantial debt structure—we borrowed and borrowed and borrowed) is covered by life insurance. We have health insurance on all our employees—most are Christian, but some not—health and everything else, including for Jayne and myself. We're rather conservative about insurance. As for insurance beyond that, on our automobiles and things like that, we have normal coverage which is not the minimum, but definitely not the maximum. We trust God for all those areas in our life, but we've tried to reach a balance, thinking of who we are and how the world would treat us if God allowed us to get in serious financial trouble.

David Pullen: I think I was one who made the comments—but I don't think I'd make a doctrine or a major theory out of it. Insurance has been a point of wrestling for us. Being in a two-person firm with no employees other than a secretary being dependent on us means that a group plan wouldn't work. For us, medical insurance would cost in the neighborhood of about $900 per year. I don't think most people realize what their employer is paying out. I know from a government unit I talked to that the fringe benefits that go into retirement pension, insurance, things like that, come to almost as much as the actual salary itself. As we've wrestled with that, where we have come down is that it's just a question of . . . is there to be equality among God's people? For us—just as an example of something, maybe it's just a burden that God has given—am I going to be facing the same risks that most of the world faces routinely?

The medical services are available to us, but what we are worried about is paying for them with insurance. For most of the world, the service isn't even available. They've got to trust God for the healing as well as for paying for it if they can get it. For us, at least at this point, we're just having to face it. It's scary—if something happened to me as the wage earner, we'd be in a pickle. That's all there is to it. The one answer I've had, when people have raised the question, "Well so-and-so had to learn the lesson with their philosophy on insurance, when others had to come to their rescue ..." is that I think that can be good for the Body on occasion. The other thing, which I guess we might realize if we got into a pickle, is that God can provide. Sometimes he blesses others so they can be in a position to provide for our needs. That would be a way of *all* of God's people being brought into the act together. We would be dependent on each other.

My wife Nancy Jo had an aunt who became sick who didn't have insurance. She had given her whole life for Houghton College—that was all she had done, she had never married. When she got sick, the nieces and nephews had to help out, and that was something that was used as an example for me to struggle with. It didn't take much struggling to come to the conclusion that God had blessed them so that they would be in a position to help her out when she had that need. I'm not sure she had done anything wrong in having to be dependent on them for that love to flow. I think there is a lot we can learn in these areas.

EVANGELISM AND SIMPLER LIFESTYLE

Gladys M. Hunt

7

"This new reality [entering the kingdom of God] places men [and women] in a position of crisis—they cannot continue to live as if nothing had happened; the Kingdom of God demands a new mentality, a reorientation of all their values, repentance.... The change imposed involves a new lifestyle."[1]

The gospel demands change. New life, new lifestyle. Evangelism is not the preaching of a new lifestyle. It is the preaching of new life; it is the good news about Jesus. Lifestyle is another matter. Logically and ethically it is the fruit of the good news naturally and purposefully enhancing the evangel. We want to examine here the relationship between lifestyle and the preaching of the good news.

WHAT IS A SIMPLE LIFESTYLE?

I must confess to great confusion of mind and heart when I ask, What is a simple lifestyle? Simple compared to what? H. L. Hunt, the Texas multimillionaire, carried sandwiches to lunch in a brown bag every day—sandwiches made of bread made from wheat from his fields, ground and baked in his kitchen. The seats in the leather chairs in his office sagged and the living room in his home overlooking the lake in downtown Dallas wore a dingy 1930 beige. Did he live a simple lifestyle? Or was frugality merely part of his eccentricity? And what cause prompted his penurious ways?

Another person receives acclaim for driving an ordinary Ford (and that one four years old) while others in his income bracket drive Cadillacs and Lincolns. Certainly that is simpler and less ostentatious.

Another shops at five different supermarkets to get the best prices. Or haunts the thrift shop periodically to get good used clothing. Or scours the bins behind supermarkets to salvage food that has been tossed out. Is that what we mean by a simple lifestyle?

Or what of the mother who tears apart an old skirt, laboriously clipping all the stitches, pressing out the seams, fitting the patterns to make a new skirt for her smaller daughter. Time-consuming, yes. But wasteful, no. Is that what it means to have a simple lifestyle? And what do such things have to do with evangelism?

I could go on. Simplicity takes many shapes and forms. No fertilizer for the lawn. Moving to the country and growing your own vegetables and cutting wood for your fires. Biking instead of driving. Baking instead of buying. Freebies for entertainment.

Two problems distort discussions about simple lifestyle: a tendency to legalism which leads to pride, and an inadequate theology about possessions. Legalism wants a monolithic style. During the late 60s I invited a campus rebel to our

home for further conversations (which were later incor-
porated in a book on contemporary student opinions called
Listen to Me). When he arrived in our ticky-tacky subdivi-
sion and rang the bell, almost his first words were "I'm surprised to find you living here." He had his idea of where
someone who thought the way I did should live: a flat near
campus like his—with plants in the windows instead of cur-
tains, pillows on the floor and one shadeless lamp in the cor-
ner, complete with onion smells wafting up the stairwell.
How could I possibly live where I live with all the needs in
the world? It was simply not appropriate to live in a subdivi-
sion. He seemed not to consider his high rent, magnificent
stereo, record collection, ten-speed bike and the cost of just-
right jeans. Concern for the world, it seems, must have a certain look, a certain style.

Simple lifestyle in those terms becomes faddish, almost
cultic. And of course some of the protestors of the late 60s
and early 70s have joined the establishment and are now
accumulating the "good life."

Simple lifestyle is not a way to cop out of social relationships and responsibilities. Many of the specifics that mark
simplicity might also mark selfishness or a stingy spirit.
Phyllis McGinley in her book *Sixpence in Her Shoe* explains
it delightfully:

> *Thrift is neither selfishness nor cheese-paring, but a large,
> compassionate attribute, a just regard for God's material
> gifts. It has nothing in common with meanness and is dif-
> ferent even from economy, which, although it may assist
> thrift, is a habit rather than a moral act.... Economy
> saves pennies, trims corners, and has a tidy mind.... The
> poor receive economy's handouts, but they will be relent-
> lessly entered on a tax return. Meanness ruthlessly stints
> the table, lets others pay the check, and when it gives old
> coats to refugee committees, cuts off buttons and fur col-
> lars. Thrift is something else again. When thrift serves*

stew to the family to ease the budget, it sees to it that the dish is savory as filet mignon and it delights to share with anyone who comes to the door. It is never stingy and ant-like. Thrift is a preserver rather than a hoarder and rejoices in hospitality.[2]

We should be sure, then, that our discussion of simplicity in lifestyle first means a lifestyle-for-others—simple so that it can truly honor others and meet their needs. As one woman said, "Life is too short to stuff a mushroom."

Second, our theology gets tangled in emotions. We feel guilty because we wonder if we are possessed by our possessions. We suspect that is true, but we lack the courage to investigate reality. Our view of God is bound to affect us. Is he an austere, parsimonious Being who wants to take away all that is beautiful and comfortable, a kind of bare-room monastic God? After all, the Son of man had no place to lay his head. He never married. He borrowed a donkey when he needed it. He fished for money. Others supplied his needs, but he did have a robe good enough for soldiers to gamble for it at the foot of the cross. So what conclusions do you want to draw?

Some people assert that the Scriptures say very clearly that God has given us all things richly to enjoy. Human prosperity is the blessing of God. He who gave elaborate instructions for the building of the temple with its intricate work of gold and silver, its carvings. He is the one who has placed in us a love of the beautiful, and has sanctioned our personal collection of some of the good things of this world. It is true that God is extravagant with both beauty and joy. He is almost wasteful with seedpods, butterflies and sunsets. Imagine a God who gives ten verses in the book of Job to the glory of the hippopotamus and thirty-four verses to the crocodile. Imagine a God who gifts a Bach and a Beethoven to conceive such magnificent sounds. He makes artists and poets. "Glory be to God for dappled things," Gerard Manley Hopkins wrote.

But God is also willing to lay down glory. He humbled himself, took on human form and became obedient—even to death on a cross. He gave his life for ours, that we might know his righteousness.

So what does glory and humility have to do with lifestyle? I prefer to talk about *obedient lifestyle* rather than simple lifestyle. We are not committed to simplicity. We are committed to the Lord of the universe. Can those who claim to know him not care about what is on his heart?

To be unconcerned that our rising affluence is crippling already poverty-stricken nations should be unthinkable. One-third of the world's population consumes three-fourths of the world's protein every year, and we are part of that one-third. A different third of the world's people has an annual per capita income of $100 or less. We cannot ignore the cry of hungry neighbors.

But we dare not be unconcerned about spiritual famine either. Our spiritual lifestyle is often as extravagant as our material lifestyle. A kind of spiritual greed for experiences, a euphoria about truth, has thousands going from conference to convention and across town to another meeting. Many Christians live in a cozy subculture enjoying group-think.

We are often as oblivious to empty hearts around us as we are to empty stomachs. All around us—in our neighborhoods, our cities, across our country and around the world—are people with hollow hearts. They have simply never heard the evangel.

The purpose of this paper is to examine the relationship between a simple lifestyle and evangelism. How can a simple lifestyle enhance, encourage, aid, hasten, affect evangelism?

A SIMPLE DEFINITION OF EVANGELISM

John R. W. Stott gives a simple definition of evangelism: "Evangelism is sharing the good news with others. The good news is Jesus. And the good news about Jesus which we announce is that he died for our sins and was raised from death and that in consequence he reigns as Lord and Savior at God's right hand, and has the authority both to command repentance and faith, and to bestow forgiveness of sins and the gift of the Spirit on all those who repent, believe and are baptized."[3]

I believe that biblical evangelism is adequately defined by Stott's statement, although I'm aware that some would include additional elements in such a definition. That is not to say that evangelism meets all of a person's needs in God's sight. As Bishop John Taylor has said, "A hungry man has no ears." Hungry people need physical bread. Scripture is clear: "If anyone has material possessions and sees his brother in need but has no pity on him, how can the love of God be in him?" (1 Jn. 3:17 NIV). Biblical evangelism is not in opposition to meeting social needs. As Ron Sider says in his monograph *Evangelism, Salvation and Social Justice*, evangelism and social action are equal and full partners in the mission of God's people. Both are necessary. Neither is an excuse for the other. Each stands in its own right. Each demands presence to some degree, but action, servanthood and communication must accompany meaningful presence in either.

Evangelism is simple obedience. Jesus told us to *go, tell, teach.* Social action is simple obedience too. Together they are a full-orbed expression of discipleship. People are not bodiless souls or soulless bodies. We must try to be as holistic as our earthbound vision allows us to be.

The Lausanne Covenant states that "in the church's mission of sacrificial service evangelism is primary." Our purpose here is not to argue the validity of that statement but to underscore that human beings without Christ are without hope in this world and the next, that alienation from God has eternal consequences. That fact needs to grip us until we hurt a little, not so that we frenetically assume God's responsibility but that we willingly obey the Commander.

PRACTICAL ISSUES

The Commander has the program. He is ultimately the enabler. Has he, in fact, enabled us to do something about the evangelization of the world?

First, and most obviously, we can personally obey his command to evangelize. Generally we want to respond in every way but that: give, send, pray. If every believer "gossiped" the gospel out of a convinced heart at every opportunity, the evangelization of the world would be well on its way. Until simple obedience is our first concern, our primary need is for repentance.

Second, we can fund a great army of those who will preach the good news. Why is the church of Jesus Christ allowing young people to itinerate the length and breadth of the land with a tin cup, as it were, pleading for support to allow them the privilege of going to share the message? They have been trained; they are ready to go. What delays their going? They have not raised their support. Why isn't the church out looking for those who will go, ready with funds, already having prayed that the Lord would send forth laborers?

Instead we find travel-weary candidates, beholden to hundreds of supporters, spending too much time cultivating contacts to bring in dollars that will allow them to obey God's call. That happens regularly in independent mission boards and increasingly with denominational boards. It is called the personal touch, justified because it works and because of the prayer support supposedly engendered by the contacts. But it also encourages a personality cult. The man or woman fit for tribal work may have a quiet, persevering way, not given to public speaking or easy social expression. It may take such a person twice as long to raise support.

Pragmatically, raising one's own support "works," which keeps people from asking if it is according to truth. It encourages the church to feel benevolent when the church has, in fact, been penurious. It fosters a double standard: one standard of living for believers who go and another standard of living for believers who stay at home. What would happen if the members of the body voluntarily assumed a minimum standard of living (not legislated, but decided before God individually) and gave the rest of their income to the mission of the church in the world? The first thing that would happen would be the revelation of our idols—do we serve God or mammon? And that would bless us all.

Fuzzy thinking about commitment has to be dealt with if the church is to obey the command to go and tell. Os Guinness in his book *In Two Minds* speaks of people who move smoothly through three levels of understanding and still leave out something essential. It is possible for persons to know their need, to know that Christianity provides an answer and that Christianity is true, and still believe inadequately because they have never fully committed themselves to Christ.[4] Our Lord Jesus knew that our view of earthly possessions most clearly defines our commitment. It did with the rich young ruler. He went away sorrowful for he had many possessions.

The means to reach the world might be in hand if believers simply tithed. "The gulf between what affluent Northern Christians give and what they *could* give is a terrifying tragedy. *Christianity Today* reported recently that a mere tithe from the fifty-two largest U.S. denominations would be $17.5 billion annually. Instead they gave only $4.4 billion in *total church giving* in 1971."[5] "Total church giving" is not necessarily money to help either the poor or the unevangelized. Suppose the church gave $17.5 billion; that would still be only a tithe. We need to break through with fresh urgency. Even the Old Testament economy of the law had tithes and *offerings;* surely the economy of grace urges us to explore more than tithes. "Freely you have received, freely give"

(Mt. 10:8 NIV). God holds us as accountable for what we keep for ourselves as for what we give. Jesus still stands by the treasury.

The amount of money that would be available for a needy world if all believers scaled down their standard of living excites the imagination. Glory would be given to the name of God not only from the expansion of his kingdom but from the purifying of it. What hinders believers from the carefree lifestyle Jesus was talking about in the Sermon on the Mount ("Take no thought . . .")? Is it that we derive our sense of well-being from what we possess? Do our possessions reassure us of our worth? Surely that is sub-Christian thinking. Is it anxiety about the future? It is true that God is not honored by a failure to plan, but he is less honored by unbelief. How much it must please God when those who say they know him then trust him with their lives and possessions.

Third, we can rethink our strategy and let go of our money. The church and individuals often give gifts that are not truly gifts. We want to control what we give. We have strings attached. Some feedback, some strokes are necessary to make us feel good about giving. Our money can be used for *this* but not for *that*. I am not suggesting careless or thoughtless giving. Hard-nosed evaluation of strategy and quality of work marks godly giving. We need prayerful planning, not simply impulse giving (yet pity the person who never feels the impulse of the Spirit to do something spontaneous). What I am saying is that if the world is to be evangelized we have to expand our vision of who will do it and how it will be done and let go our money to do it. We need to ask how the job can best be done.

Waves of change continually affect the missionary enterprise. Americans today cannot go to some places; we are not the best choices to send to others. But we are often woefully provincial in our concern for the world. We pray appropriately for our missionaries, our denominational outreach, or whatever. And there it ends. We need to pray for the whole church—for the planting of the church, the growth of the church, the health of the church. Who prays for the places where we can't send anyone? Who will use the news of the world as a prayer reminder? We must rid ourselves of a colonial attitude, of any trace of benefactor—and we must be willing to use our resources wherever the need is.

For instance, I am impressed with the project undertaken by the Langham Trust fund, where key African and Asian nationals receive support in theological training in England to further the work of the church in their country. Or the Jubilee Fund which provides support for national mission development in various places in the world, keeping believers in their area and sharing the gospel.

The new evangelical seminary in Central Africa Empire may well provide a key to evangelizing Francophone Africa. That seminary is the vision of an African leader, Byang Kato. Who supports such a broad venture in an area where the church is weak and barely supports its own pastors? Or what of the evangelical seminary outside Paris, which meets an urgent need for first-rate education for French pastors?

Assam has closed to missionaries. Nationals have taken over all the facets of work once done by Baptist General Conference missionaries. The church is young and needs teaching to face the persecution it now is experiencing. The BGC is supporting Assamese broadcasts and Assamese personnel to broadcast from Sri Lanka. *Africa Enterprise* supports African evangelists, helps needy refugees in the name of Christ, supplies money so that Ugandan Christian students who are studying abroad can complete their education and be ready to return home when the present trial is past. The list could go on.

The creative possibilities are far greater than anything we know about. We need to release funds to internationally supervised programs or to projects devised by nationals which meet legitimate needs and which could further the work of evangelism in an indigenous way.

Someone will warn about the danger of "rice" Christians, those who might respond to the gospel because of the offer of food or shelter. Not at all! We need to trust the national church, not cripple it. I believe we have not been nearly creative enough in working closely with national leaders to equip their own people in the work of evangelism.

Beyond that we need a fresh call to incarnate the gospel wherever the Lord calls us personally. We have allowed our need of possessions and the finery of life to separate us from the neighbors in our own communities. We salve our conscience by giving to a missionary offering instead of sharing the gospel with a neighbor. Visions of lands far off; blindness for those at home. The love of things can keep us from going across the street or to any other hard place to obey Christ. Yet he remains the supreme example—that laying aside of what was rightfully his and humbling himself to become obedient.

Our possessions make us increasingly immobile. The idea of incarnating the gospel in primitive circumstances is hard. The problems of health, sanitation and safety in the slums of the world's cities threaten those who go to live among them. It may be that some will die, which society will call tragic wastefulness. Mother Teresa took the risk of not developing immunities, as did Granny Brand in India. Our confidence in a God who counts such "waste" as fragrant worship needs to increase. We need to ask that great biblical question, Is anything too hard for God?

Does living in the inner city or the wrong neighborhood for the sake of Jesus strain God's ability to take care of his own? Our possessions may be pilfered by the people we are trying to reach. The more we have, the greater the risk. Our best efforts may be spurned, our person mistreated. Is that too much for God or us? Many more need to stay in changing neighborhoods or to live in the hard places at home for Jesus' sake.

Think how many American Christians live in spacious homes with perfect decor—sterile places where few outsiders are ever welcome. Unused rooms, unused clothes in the closets, a freezer full of food, tennis rackets, bikes, soft drinks by the carton—and a tight social schedule that doesn't allow time for people who live in other spacious homes on the same street. Lost people include those who are poor and those who are rich and those who are in middle-class America. Our hospitals, nursing homes, retirement centers, jails, juvenile homes and shelters for runaways and battered wives —all are full of desperately hurting people. Some people don't need to move; they need to open their eyes, unclutter their lives, empty their closets and open their homes for Jesus' sake and share his goodness and love. The need to communicate the gospel is not limited to any geographical location. Only our vision is limited.

In many places the witness of the gospel needs to be strengthened by the demonstration of a community, a community that lives and preaches the good news about Jesus. I believe specialized ministries like that are carried on effectively in large cities across the world, and their number could increase. The words of one support the testimony of another. Openness of lifestyle invites others into the center of the community to show a drastically different way to think about life.

My point is this. Our obsession with the material world can paralyze our best intents. It takes time and energy to maintain and enjoy too many possessions. Concern for a needy world, a world that dies for lack of knowledge of Christ, becomes the least of our concerns. Dom Helder Camara in *Revolution through Peace* says, "I know how very hard it is to be rich and still keep the milk of human kindness. Money has a dangerous way of putting scales on one's eyes, a dangerous way of freezing people's hands, eyes, lips and hearts."[6]

I know this too, and I mourn my earthiness, my frozen hands, eyes, lips and heart. We all need to hear again our Lord Jesus say, "I am the light of the world. He who follows me will not walk in darkness, but will have the light of life. . . . If the Son makes you free, you will be free indeed" (Jn. 8: 12, 36). And then we need to realize that we have been made *light* in a needy world and pray that we will have the freedom to use our possessions in spreading of light, instead of being used up by them.

Notes
[1]René Padilla in *Let the Earth Hear His Voice,* ed. J. D. Douglas (Minneapolis: Worldwide Publications, 1975), p. 128.
[2]Phyllis McGinley, *Sixpence in Her Shoe,* (New York: Dell Pub. Co., 1965), pp. 80-81.
[3]John R. W. Stott, *Christian Mission in the Modern World* (Downers Grove, Ill.: InterVarsity Press, 1975), pp. 34-35.
[4]Os Guinness, *In Two Minds* (Downers Grove, Ill.: InterVarsity Press, 1976), p. 121.
[5]Ronald J. Sider, *Rich Christians in an Age of Hunger* (Downers Grove, Ill.: InterVarsity Press, 1977), p. 187.
[6]Dom Helder Camara, *Revolution through Peace* (New York: Harper & Row, 1971).

THE SOCIO-ECONOMIC-POLITICAL ORDER AND OUR LIFESTYLES

George N. Monsma, Jr.

8

Although this paper deals with the influence of the socio-economic-political order (or "institutions") on economic lifestyles (hereafter simply "lifestyles") in rich and poor countries, it should be made clear at the outset that individuals' attitudes and behavior are *also* important determinants of differences in lifestyles. Within any set of institutions (or structures and policies) there will be opportunities for many people to adopt a variety of lifestyles, ranging from those that show great concern for their neighbors (in the biblical sense of those that stand in need of their help) to those that show no such concern.

The socio-economic-political order is itself the result of the attitudes and behavior of those in the various societies of the world. On the other hand, the institutions have an important influence on lifestyles since they set boundaries for the choices of lifestyle by individuals (and families), and because they also influence the attitudes and behavior of individuals.

Proper institutions and proper behavior and attitudes within them are complements in attaining proper lifestyles. The less *just* either institutions or behaviors are, the greater is the burden placed on the other. The more that individuals or groups strive for superiority over others, the more stringent the institutions will have to be in order to insure opportunity for all. And the more stringent and detailed the structures and policies become, the less scope there is for responsible (as well as irresponsible) individual decision making and action, and the greater probability there is for inequitable side effects.

Where lifestyles are irresponsible, Christians should work for changes in both individual attitudes and behavior and in the socio-economic-political order in attempts to achieve more justice. As Ronald Sider has amply illustrated, the Lord, when instituting the socio-economic-political order for Israel, did not leave it up to individual actions to provide all families with the opportunity to be free from poverty, but created institutions which would have that effect on a regular basis (e.g., the laws concerning the year of Jubilee, and restrictions on slavery, loans and the harvesting of fields).[1]

One of the most important ways that the socio-economic-political order influences lifestyles is through its influence on the distribution of income, both within and between societies, because income differences are the most important determinants of lifestyle differences. Therefore institutional determinants of income differences within the United States, between high-income and low-income countries, and within low-income countries will be examined. But the institutions of a society also affect lifestyles by influencing how incomes are spent, which will also be considered.

INSTITUTIONAL INFLUENCES ON LIFESTYLE IN THE UNITED STATES[2]

1. Distribution of Income. A family's income in a capitalistic society is limited to the sum of the resources (wealth) the family owns and offers for use in the economy, times the respective market values of those resources. There are large variations in the amount and market value of the resources owned by various families. In any capitalistic society that variation is modified somewhat by taxation and non-market transfers of income, but wide disparities in income remain. It is useful to distinguish between two general categories of wealth: physical wealth (including financial wealth) and human wealth. Physical wealth is the total current value of all the physical goods and claims on goods a family owns, including (but not limited to) land, homes, automobiles, stocks, bonds and money. In a market economy that value is based on the current value of the expected net income that those resources could provide, now and in the future, and on the risks associated with them. Human wealth (often called human capital) is what the current value of the family members' net earnings, current and future, would be if they could be sold at the present time. Of course no markets exist for such sales; that is, we do not allow people to sell themselves or others into slavery. That creates an important distinction between physical and human wealth—the former can be sold and the money obtained used to buy something else, but the latter cannot. That gives a greater flexibility to holders of physical capital. But since the labor value of individuals does differ widely, and a person's labor value can be modified by certain expenditures (e.g., on education or health care), it is helpful to have a concept such as human capital or wealth. (Human capital is, of course, in no way an indication of the ultimate worth or value of persons as human beings, or of their actual benefit to others.)

Since there are no markets for human wealth, it would be

very difficult, if not impossible, to measure accurately its distribution (only a general indication can be obtained from the distribution of labor incomes). Thus the statistics we do have on the distribution of wealth are limited to physical wealth. Even the distribution of physical wealth is difficult to estimate; there have been relatively few studies of wealth distribution in the United States and the statistics that do exist are probably subject to considerable error. But based on a 1962 survey by the Federal Reserve Board it has been estimated that the wealthiest 1 percent of consumer units in the United States owned 33 percent of the total wealth, the wealthiest 5 percent owned 53 percent, and the wealthiest 20 percent owned 77 percent of the total wealth. On the other hand, the least wealthy 20 percent had no net wealth, that is, their liabilities exceeded their assets. The concentration of wealth-holdings differs by type of wealth. It is most equal for those types that give relatively little economic power, for example, homes and automobiles, and it is least equal for those types which give a great deal of economic power, for example, corporate stocks. It was estimated that in 1962 the wealthiest 1 percent of consumer units owned 62 percent of the corporate stock, the wealthiest 5 percent owned 86 percent, and the wealthiest 20 percent owned 97 percent of the corporate stock.[3]

Since the holdings of physical wealth are so unevenly distributed, the vast majority of families must rely on the labor of their members for almost all of their income (i.e., on the returns to their human wealth). Although labor incomes are more equally distributed than non-labor incomes, there is still a great disparity in them reflecting differences in productivity and market power between different individuals. Persons who have a high level of education or training, or are members of a strong union or a professional organization that has been able to restrict entry into its profession (e.g., the American Medical Association), are apt to have higher levels of labor income (and more job security), on average, than others. The labor income of specific persons may vary according to things beyond their control, for example the profitability of a company they work for or changes in the demand for the skills they have acquired. If the head of a family has had only a low level of education, is ill or disabled, is over 65, is non-white, or is a woman, the family has a much-greater-than-average likelihood of being poor, because the labor of such people tends to have a low market value when they are in the labor force, and often they are not in the labor force because of personal situation (e.g., illness or child-care responsibility) or market restrictions (e.g., discrimination or mandatory retirement). Unemployment rates are also higher for those groups, so they have the double disadvantage of earning less, on average, while they are working, and being involuntarily without work more often.[4]

Since those who have the most physical capital also tend to have the highest labor incomes, the inequalities of income are compounded. The result is that while the average income in the United States is well above the amount necessary for an adequate lifestyle, we have many families in the United States that do not have enough income to provide for the basic necessities of life, such as adequate nutrition, clothing, housing and medical care, to say nothing of enough to function in society over a period of time.

Such inequities are even more serious because they tend to be self-perpetuating over time. Children born into a relatively rich family will generally receive more gifts and bequests of physical capital, both before and after they become economically independent, than will children born into a relatively poor family. Even more important, in most cases, is the fact that children in the wealthier family will receive much more human capital before (and also after) they enter the labor market, and thus are apt to have much higher labor incomes. That greater human capital comes from the fact that they generally receive better nutrition and health care, and more and better formal and informal education. For example, the public schools in high-income areas tend to have more and better staffs and facilities than those in low-income areas, and more higher-income families send their children to superior private schools; also the probability of college attendance is over twice as high for children of parents with a high socio-economic status than for those of parents with a low socio-economic status, even when ability is taken into account.[5] Children from a high-income family will, on average, associate with adults and other children who have had more and better education, which will help their own learning considerably; and they will have many more "role-models" of "successful" persons, which will tend to give more motivation for working hard within the system, in and out of school. Such things all raise the potential market value of their labor. Children from the wealthier families will also tend to have more contacts helpful in obtaining high-paying jobs, which will often enable them to obtain a greater return on their human capital. In addition, the higher one's existing wealth and income are, the easier it is to save and thus accumulate more.

An individual's income is of course influenced to some extent by individual effort and ability; those factors are often important but they are not the only factors important in achieving a moderate or high income, and they alone are not enough. It is extremely difficult, and not always possible, for those growing up in a poor family, faced as they often are by poor nutrition, poor health care, poor housing and poor education, few useful contacts in job markets and no financial or physical capital to help them, to develop their God-given talents to such a degree that when they are adults they can adequately function in society (i.e., have regular and meaningful work, provide adequately for their families, be able to aid others who are in need, have potential influence on governments as they affect them, etc.). That is especially true for those who are members of a racial minority faced with pervasive discrimination in education, housing, employment and other areas.

The disparities in income that result from such institutions are obvious from the statistics regarding the distribution of income in the United States. For although the average (mean) family income was over $18,000 in 1977, there were still almost 25 million persons (11.6 percent of the population) living in households with incomes below the official poverty line (U.S. Bureau of the Census, 1978). The poverty line was about $6,200 for a non-farm family of four in 1977. That certainly represents severe poverty in most areas of the country. In recent years there have also been over 20 million persons in households with incomes between 100 and 150 percent of the official poverty line, incomes which are very low for a family to attempt to function within the United States today (for an average-sized family the upper limit of that range is about 50 percent of the average family income).

Looking at the distribution of income in another way, in 1977 the 20 percent of the families with the lowest incomes received only 5.2 percent of the total national family income, whereas the highest-income 20 percent received 41.5 percent of the total income (eight times as much), and the top 5 percent of families received 15.7 percent of the income (over eleven times as much per family).[6]

It is clear from such statistics that many persons have incomes far in excess of what they need (and it should be clear to anyone who looks at American society that many consume far more than they need), while at the same time many receive less than the amount required for them to meet their basic needs. We should not quiet our consciences with the assumption that taxation and transfers take care of the problem. Taxation, taken as a whole, is roughly proportional to income in the United States (progressive taxes are made less progressive by the existence of many loopholes and are offset by regressive taxes, such as sales and payroll taxes, which take a higher proportion of low incomes than of high incomes).[7] Cash transfers are included in the income statistics given above; they are of help to many of the poor, but they are restricted in such a way that many of the poor receive no cash transfers at all, and they are so low that many of the recipients remain in poverty. Emphasis has been placed on social insurance programs (e.g., social security and unemployment insurance) which are designed to keep the nonpoor from falling into poverty, rather than on programs to raise those in poverty out of it. (Some major non-cash transfers such as food stamps and medicaid are not included in the above statistics, but even with them many families remain poor by any reasonable definition.)

The above data on income give an indication of the opportunities for consumption that families have. But poverty and economic lifestyle include more than just consumption. One might define poverty as a lack of opportunities to fulfill the responsibilities God has given a person (or family). If that is the definition, then in order to eliminate economic poverty all must have access to enough income to be able to consume the basic necessities of life. But eliminating economic poverty also requires that all families have an opportunity to develop and use their God-given talents and resources in such a way that they can provide for themselves (at least in the long run) and help others who are in need, and that all families have enough economic and political freedom to enable them to exercise responsible stewardship of their resources (including the opportunity for responsible decision making in the area of production as well as consumption).[8]

Opportunities for developing and using their talents and resources in order to become self-supporting are not available to all families in our society (recall the high levels of unemployment that are common, especially among minorities and those with little education). Government policies to deal with such problems are woefully inadequate (they include job training and special employment programs such as CETA). And very often public services important for the development of labor resources, such as education, are poorest in the very areas where the need is greatest—the low-income areas.

Opportunities for responsible, independent decision making in the productive use of their resources are even more limited for most families. Unless a family has a significant amount of non-human capital, its members have little choice but to work for someone else in order to earn an income; usually they will have little ability to influence the policies of the companies (or other organizations) for which they work. In our economic system, legal control of companies is almost always vested in the suppliers of physical capital, i.e., the "owners," rather than being shared with the suppliers of others' resources, particularly those who supply labor, i.e., the employees. That lack of power of the workers is true even when unions are present, since many of the important decisions of a company (e.g., what to produce and how to price and promote it) are held to be outside the scope of mandatory collective bargaining by our labor legislation. Since physical capital is so unequally distributed, most families do not have enough capital to start a viable small business by themselves or in cooperation with a few others. That makes it very difficult for workers to exercise responsible stewardship over their labor, insuring that it is being used in the best possible way to advance the kingdom of God. Of course many workers have alternative job opportunities and can attempt to choose the position best suited for a proper use of their talents. But the variety of job opportunities is probably directly related to wealth (physical and human), leaving the poor with little or no choice. In addition, once a person has been in a job for some time there are often considerable barriers to changing jobs, should the conditions of work change. Such barriers include loss of seniority and difficulty in obtaining another job at an older age, especially one at other than a low, entry level. Thus while most workers are not as limited in their options as the Hebrew slaves (who were to be treated as hired servants), they certainly do not have the opportunities for responsible stewardship that the independent farmer in Israel had, and that was the norm set down for the nation. Our current laws allow concentrations of physical capital to be passed along from generation to generation in many cases (because of loopholes in the inheritance tax laws), and there are no mechanisms for regularly providing the poor with enough capital to be independent stewards of their resources.[9]

2. Other Influences on Lifestyles. Even though the basic distribution of income is very unequal, there could be a more equal distribution of consumption (and production) opportunities within (and between) societies if those with high income and wealth chose voluntarily to give major portions of their income and wealth to those with less; that is not done by most such people. Of course a major cause of that is sinful self-centeredness—we love ourselves more than God and our neighbor. But social and economic institutions also play a role. Although economists tend to ignore the fact, once the basic physical necessities are obtained, individual (or family) consumption-behavior is strongly influenced by social conditions; the higher the average level of consumption in a society (or in a family's "reference group" within a society), the greater the "perceived needs" of the average family, and the higher the perceived needs, the higher the level of consumption. Thus as society becomes more affluent, most families require a higher level of consumption to maintain the same level of self-perceived happiness or well-being.[10] The variation in consumption levels probably plays a role; the high levels of consumption by some in a society probably contribute to increases in consumption by others as they try to rise to the "standard" set by the affluent. That adds to the importance of a simple lifestyle for affluent Christians; by consuming less not only will we have more to give to those in need, but we will be a visible "reference group" for others who are trying to resist the materialistic, consumption-oriented idolatry of our age.

Social forces other than emulation contribute to higher consumption levels in affluent societies. Once basic physical needs are met, many of the goods we consume are "positional" goods rather than purely private goods; that is, they affect relations to others in the society and are of such a nature that a person must spend more to get the same level of benefit if others are spending more.[11] An example is education, to the extent that it is used as a screening device by employers in allocating jobs.[12] As the general level of education rises in any society, the educational requirements for many jobs also rise, so that a person aspiring to a certain job will have to spend more (time and money) on education in order to qualify for it (think of how many jobs in the United States that required at most an eighth-grade education forty years ago require a high-school education today, and so forth on up the educational scale). That leads to higher levels of consumption as people attempt to maintain their real level of benefits, even if they do not try to increase them.

As society becomes more technologically complex, functioning in it often requires a higher level of expenditure. As Thorstein Veblen said, "invention is the mother of necessity" in many cases.[13] For example, with the invention and common usage of the automobile has come a deterioration of public transportation in many areas, and the separation of employment locations from residential areas. That often makes the ownership of an automobile a near necessity for most families in many areas of the United States. Or with the spread of refrigerators to most households, refrigeration has become more of a necessity because local markets where one can shop daily for perishable items are no longer present in many areas. The rising technological complexity of production, and the increasing size of many producing units, often make it more difficult for a family or small group of families to engage in an independent production enterprise, and add to pressures on those in such enterprises to accumulate more capital for their own use.

Further levels of consumption are almost certainly influenced by the pervasiveness of (tax-deductible) advertising[14] and by the availability and promotion of credit for consumers. We are regularly encouraged by credit suppliers to indulge our desires for goods, even if we do not currently have the money to buy them. That has led to record high levels of consumer debt and personal bankruptcies.[15]

In such ways, then, the socio-economic-political order in affluent countries influences people to use their resources for themselves, rather than sharing them with others who have greater needs; that, together with the wide disparities in income, leads to wide disparities in lifestyles, both within and between countries.

INFLUENCES OF INTERNATIONAL INSTITUTIONS ON LIFESTYLES

1. Distribution of Income. Differences in wealth and income, and thus disparities in lifestyles, are even greater between countries than they are within countries. In 1976, 1.3 billion persons lived in countries classified as "low-income" by the Overseas Development Council, countries where the average GNP (gross national product) per capita in 1974 was only $152; another 1.1 billion lived in "lower-middle-income" countries, with an average GNP per capita of $338, about one-half billion in "upper-middle-income" countries with an average GNP per capita of $1,091, and slightly more than 1 billion in "high-income" countries with an average GNP per capita of $4,361 (in the United States it was $6,670).[16] (When I speak of low-income countries in this paper I am generally referring to those in the first three groups, although at times I will distinguish between low-income and middle-income countries. Such nations are often called "developing" nations, but since all nations are developing in good or bad ways I have not used that term. Nor have I used the term "less-developed" countries since the degree of development should not be judged exclusively or even primarily by GNP per capita.) The Overseas Development Council has also worked out a "Physical Quality of Life" index based on average life expectancy, infant mortality and literacy rates. The value of that index varies considerably among countries at similar average income levels, but as income rises there is a clear and pronounced rise in the average value of the index for the groups of countries: the low-income countries average 39, the middle-income groups, 59 and 67, and the high-income countries, 95.[17] A major reason for the high death and illiteracy rates in many low-income countries is lack of resources (including both physical and human capital) and thus limited capabilities for provision of basic necessities (including food, medical care and education). Uneven distribution of resources within countries is also important.

Why are such great disparities between nations—disparities much greater than those allowed to exist in any affluent country, capitalist or socialist—allowed to exist internationally? Robert Heilbroner suggests that economic growth lies at the root of the social acceptance of affluent systems, both capitalist and socialist. He further suggests that capacities for love and concern (for identification with others) are quite limited for most people. In fact he says that those capacities are insufficient for broad support of political policies which require giving up a significant portion of economic growth to aid people distant from the givers in space, culture, race, nationality or time.[18] That should not be surprising to Christians who know that sinful people are self-centered; however we should be proclaiming by our deeds and words the good news of liberation in Christ from the unfulfilling, self-centered, materialistic idolatry of our age, and attempting to demonstrate to non-Christians that poverty, oppression and lack of opportunity have ill effects on all human beings, not only on those most directly suffering from them.

Self-centeredness is reflected politically in the "sovereignty" of individual nation-states, most of which are very unwilling to give up powers to international organizations.[19] Thus, for example, we find the high-income countries very unwilling to declare certain resources (such as the deep seabed) the "common heritage of humankind" and to be subject to international controls. Rather, they wish to retain the rights to exploit the resources of the world on their own terms. Of course, if the resources may be claimed by the first group to exploit them, it is clear that those from the affluent countries with the advanced technology will be the ones to benefit the most from them. The desire for national sovereignty is even stronger regarding resources located within a nation's geographic boundaries.

The limitations of concern and the stress on national sovereignty both limit the international transfer of resources from rich to poor to a level much below that occurring within any high-income country. There are no international taxes on income, wealth, extraction of minerals or anything else, and no automatic international transfers to the poor such as are found in every affluent country. Since the high-income countries control most important international economic agencies, such agencies' decisions often favor the high-income countries. For example, when the International Monetary Fund creates Special Drawing Rights (SDRs), which are newly created claims on resources, those claims are given primarily to the high-income countries, rather than being used to help the low-income countries (e.g., by giving the claims to them directly or by using them to finance commodity stabilization programs).[20]

Transfers of resources (human and physical) are very important for low-income countries, because the poorest of them, and the poorest people within them, do not have sufficient resources of their own to make rapid progress toward meeting all of their basic needs and developing their God-given talents. (Rapid economic growth of the high-income countries was often accomplished at the cost of the misery of many of their people, for example, in Great Britain during the industrial revolution and in the USSR during the Stalin era.) Transfers of resources from abroad can ease the burden of development on the people of a poor nation, although such transfers are not a sufficient guarantee that the burden will not fall on the poor.

2. Foreign Exchange. Because certain resources must be imported if rapid progress is to be made in improving the lifestyles of those in the poorest nations, a supply of foreign exchange (i.e., currencies that are acceptable to other countries in payment for imports) is necessary. Development goals have often been unmet in the past because of shortages of foreign exchange. The problem has become more severe in recent years for oil- and food-importing low-income nations whose deficits in their balance of payments have risen rapidly in face of increases in oil and food prices and decreases in demand for their output caused by recessions in the higher-income nations.[21] Unless additional foreign exchange is made available soon that will have serious effects on their ability to meet the present needs of their people and progress with further development, particularly for the lowest-income countries. Projections contained in a study by Wassily Leontief for the United Nations indicate that balance-of-payments problems for most low-income regions

will increase over the next twenty-five years if their economies grow fast enough to reduce the relative differences in
income between themselves and the higher-income nations.[22]

There are three basic sources of foreign exchange (other
than existing exchange reserves, which are minimal for most
low-income countries). One is export earnings; they may
come from primary products (i.e., agricultural goods and raw
materials with little or no processing) or manufactured products.

Even when fuels are excluded the majority of the exports
of the low-income nations are in the form of primary products.[23] It is by no means clear that the prices of primary
products are declining in the long run, relative to those of
manufactured goods,[24] as has often been suggested. Further,
the Leontief projections indicate that primary product prices
will rise relative to manufactured goods' prices in the coming
decades if there is rapid growth in the poorer nations.[25]
Nevertheless there continues to be a serious problem with
major short-term fluctuations in the prices of primary products. The prices of such products fluctuate much more than
the prices of manufactured goods, which are often produced
by large firms with significant control over the prices of
their products.[26] Low-income countries cannot reasonably
plan for their development when such a major source of
their foreign exchange fluctuates so much.[27] The lowest-
income countries have an especially hard time financing
even temporary balance-of-payments deficits due to falling
primary product receipts. Rapid fluctuations in prices also
make planning and development difficult for low-income
nations who are importers of primary products; rapid price
increases can also cause continuing inflation in high-income
countries by setting off price/wage spirals.[28]

Although the United States and other high-income countries have set up programs to stabilize the prices of certain domestically produced primary products (especially agricultural products), and have even enacted supply restrictions at times to raise the prices of such products, the United States and some of the other high-income countries have often opposed the efforts of low-income countries to enact international commodity agreements designed to stabilize and raise the prices of the most important commodities they export.[29] Experience with tin indicates that such plans can function successfully over time if both producer and consumer nations cooperate in them, and if the average price is not raised far above the market price.[30] It is more difficult to keep an agreement going which raises prices above the market level, but it is not impossible, especially if consumer nations cooperate.[31]

Lack of a buffer stock and price stabilization scheme for basic foodstuffs is particularly harmful. The current practice of the major high-income producer nations of protecting their home markets by import controls, encouraging production by means of price supports, and dumping excess production abroad at low prices when they have surpluses but selling at high prices when there are worldwide shortages harms the low-income countries in several ways. The import barriers and low-price sales of surpluses harm the development of agriculture in the low-income countries by depressing the prices that can be obtained by farmers in those countries; then when there are shortages and prices rise drastically and food aid is reduced, low-income countries must spend much scarce foreign exchange to buy food for their people. It would be far better for the surpluses to be put into grain reserves when production is high, keeping prices from falling so low as to discourage production, with the reserves available to keep prices from going up drastically when there are crop failures in major growing regions.[32]

A major barrier to the increase of low-income nations'

earnings from exports of manufactured products has been the tariff and non-tariff barriers that many of the high-income nations, including the United States, place on imports of such goods. Although there has been some easing of tariffs on products of low-income nations, trade barriers remain a serious problem, especially for the "middle-income" countries who have the capability of competing with the high-income countries in light manufactures and the processing of their raw materials. Existing trade barriers are particularly strong in areas in which lower-income countries often have a comparative advantage over higher-income countries.[33]

The World Bank has estimated that if all tariff and non-tariff barriers to exports of manufactures by low- and middle-income countries were eliminated, "the annual export earnings of the developing countries by 1985 could increase by as much as $24 billion—$21 billion of which would accrue to the middle income countries and $3 billion to the countries with per capita incomes under $200."[34] That would be a very significant increase in export earnings, since it is equal to about two-thirds of the 1974 level of exports of manufactures of those countries; it is also equal to about two-thirds of the balance-of-payments deficits of the non-oil-exporting, low-income countries in 1975, and is almost twice the net flow of Official Development Assistance (i.e., foreign aid) from the high-income, market-oriented countries to the low- and middle-income countries in 1975.[35]

Exports not only provide needed foreign exchange for the low-income nations, but they also provide additional jobs for their people, an important factor since high rates of unemployment are common in low-income countries. Trade restrictions on processed agricultural products, handicrafts and other labor-intensive goods that are likely to be produced by relatively poor persons are particularly harmful.[36] A major hindrance to reduction in trade barriers is the fact that large increases in imports often cause unemployment in the importing countries; such unemployment often affects relatively low-income workers most heavily. The high-income countries in effect "export their unemployment" by means of trade barriers; yet the high-income countries have a greater capacity for creating jobs for their people than do the low-income countries. It has been estimated that for every job lost in the United States as a result of increased imports from lower-income countries, from two to six jobs could be created in the exporting countries, taking into account only direct effects (the poorer the country, the greater the number of jobs that would be created, because of lower output per worker). And if indirect effects are included, a very poor country might gain employment for as many as twenty workers for every worker displaced in a high-income country.[37]

A second source of foreign exchange is foreign investment in low-income countries, which can take the forms of lending on market terms or private direct investment. Foreign investment is a very limited source for the poorest nations (particularly the lending), but many of the middle-income nations have raised considerable funds in that manner. For both low- and middle-income countries, however, the net outflow of earnings on previous foreign investments *exceeds* the net inflow of new capital, thus requiring foreign exchange obtained in other ways to make up the difference.[38]

The third basic source of foreign exchange is aid, that is, loans or grants from private or public sources for which repayment is either not required or is on concessional terms, with interest rates substantially below the market rates and usually with a long period for repayment. The net flow of such aid from public sources (called Official Development Assistance, or ODA) from the high-income Western donors was $13.6 billion in 1975, or an average of .36 percent of

their combined GNPs. The net flow of private assistance from
those countries was $1.3 billion, or less than .04 percent of
their combined GNPs. The net flow of ODA from the United
States in 1975 was .27 percent of GNP and the net private
flow was .05 percent of GNP; the two combined are less than
$23 per person in the U.S. (and over one-fourth of the U.S.
ODA was for "security supporting assistance," which might
more properly be considered military aid rather than eco-
nimic aid).

By contrast, Sweden gave .82 percent and the Nether-
lands .75 percent of their GNPs in ODA in 1975. The net
flow of concessional aid from the OPEC nations in 1975
totaled $2.7 billion, or 1.35 percent of their combined GNPs
(the majority of it to Arab countries), and the net flow of
ODA from the communist countries was $0.75 billion, or
less than .1 percent of GNP in 1975.[39] Thus the absence
of any international taxes and transfers results in a level of
transfer that is very low in relation to the needs of the poorest
countries, and much lower than similar transfers within
countries.

Not only is the level of transfer low, the aid has often not
been directed in such a way as to help the poorest of the
world's people. Most of the aid goes to middle-income countries rather than to the poorest countries. The use of aid has
often been restricted to the purchase of goods from the donor
countries, which often means technologies inappropriate for
the low-income countries and particularly ill-suited for
meeting the needs of the poor in them. The resulting development projects have often been highly capital-intensive,
creating only a few jobs, and contributing to the "dualization" of the economy, that is, the growth of a small, relatively high-wage "modern" sector in a country with high unemployment and low wages for the masses of people in the
"traditional" sector. Such development strategies were
based on a "trickle-down" theory of development which

held that if the GNP of a country were raised by developing a small modern sector, the benefits would spread to all population groups; such "development" has not in general contributed much to the relief of the absolute poverty of the poorest people in the world, and it exacerbates the problems of relative poverty in the countries where it occurs.[40] In particular it has done little for the poor in rural areas of low-income countries, even though more than 80 percent of the very poor in low-income countries live in rural areas.[41] In fact, such a "dual economy" strategy often increases the problems of urban poverty since the hope of a higher-paying urban job induces many more rural residents to migrate to the cities seeking jobs than can be accommodated in the cities, adding to urban unemployment and slums. Because of that, many high-income countries and international agencies have begun to shift the patterns of their aid so that it is aimed more directly at meeting the basic human needs of the poor, such as basic health care, nutrition, education and employment. An important component of that has been rural development —bringing the basic public services (health care, education, transportation, etc.) to rural areas, and providing aid to small, labor-intensive enterprises in rural areas (agricultural and otherwise).[42] But the change has by no means been complete and there is considerable resistance to it among the elite in both rich and poor nations.[43] In addition, much aid is allocated directly or indirectly to military purposes, rather than to development of opportunities for the poor. In fiscal year 1975, for example, 47 percent of total United States aid was military aid or "security supporting assistance."[44]

Offsetting aid transfers is a "brain drain" from low-income countries to high-income countries, which reduces the supply of a very important resource, trained manpower, in the low-income countries. The immigration policies of the United States and other high-income countries are an important cause of the drain, since they give preference to highly trained immigrants over others. That is, the countries with the greatest wealth of trained manpower, and the greatest capacities to train more, exclude most untrained persons while making it easier for highly trained persons to immigrate. Between 1962 and 1972 over 170,000 highly skilled persons migrated to the United States, Canada and the United Kingdom alone from the low-income countries,[45] their "imputed capital value" exceeded the aid flowing in the reverse direction.[46]

3. Transnational Enterprises. Transnational enterprises (TNEs), by their control of such a large proportion of the world's production and technology, have enormous power in the world today. Their influence extends far beyond the purely economic sphere, and in many respects they are not subject to the control of any one government. Their resources enable them to be of aid to some lower-income countries in their development plans, but the goals of the TNEs and the countries are often not the same. Unequal bargaining power between TNEs and the lower-income countries has often led to a situation in which the TNEs' activities have been of limited or even negative value to the countries in which they operate. TNEs have often contributed to "dualization" of the economies of low-income countries by bringing modern technology and products and an affluent lifestyle into the low-income countries. They have sometimes followed policies which while profitable for themselves and an elite in their "host" country, have neglected or even worsened the plight of the poor in such countries (for example, conversion of cropland from domestic food products to export products, displacing many small farmers and raising the domestic price of food). The growth in the size of TNEs contributes to a situation in which the control over decisions in the national and international economies is concentrated into fewer and fewer hands. The lack of any legally enforceable international code of behavior governing TNEs, covering such areas as maximum size, concentration and market structure, ownership and control, transfer pricing, taxation, accounting standards and disclosure, limits the control and bargaining power of low-income countries (and high-income countries) in dealing with TNEs.[47]

In summary, then, there are significant features of the international socio-economic-political order (or lack thereof) which contribute to the maintenance of large disparities in income and lifestyle between and within countries and help to perpetuate the poverty of many in low-income countries.

INSTITUTIONAL INFLUENCES ON LIFESTYLES WITHIN LOW-INCOME COUNTRIES

1. Differences between Countries. It is difficult to generalize about the institutional factors within lower-income countries which contribute to poverty and to resulting disparities in lifestyles, because conditions differ so greatly among low-income countries. The average income per capita varies a great deal among such countries; the distribution of income and degree of provision of the basic necessities of life to all differ considerably; land is extremely scarce and intensively used in some, but not in others; land is much more equally distributed in some than in others; some are net exporters of primary products, others are net importers of them; and so forth.[48] Thus any generalization is apt to have some exceptions.

2. Distribution of Income. As in the United States, control over wealth is very unequal, which leads to very unequal distributions of income in most low-income countries. In fact, in most low-income countries the distribution of income is less equal than in the United States, and of course many more suffer from a very dire absolute poverty.[49] In many low-income countries the top five percent of income recipients receive over a fifth of the total income, and in some they receive over one-half of the total income.[50] Since most of the people (and most of the poor people) live in rural areas, and since agriculture is a major source of employment and income, the distribution of land is very important to the distribution of income. Unfortunately no year of Jubilee or other land reform mechanism has been instituted in most low-income countries, so an unequal distribution of land contributes greatly to rural poverty (and indirectly via migration to urban poverty).[51] Political power is usually in the hands of those with the concentrations of wealth, making it difficult to achieve significant land reform or other wealth redistribution.

3. Confidence Mechanisms. Existence of what Charles Elliott calls confidence mechanisms or "con-mechs" also helps preserve the inequality in many low-income countries. A con-mech is a structure or policy that gives the illusion of a competitive opportunity for advancement for the less advantaged, but in reality serves primarily to help benefit the already advantaged who are in control of the con-mech. Thus con-mechs help build confidence and support for the system, at the same time that they help perpetuate disparities in opportunity, income, power and lifestyle.[52] (Con-mechs also exist in high-income countries.) An example of a con-mech commonly found in low-income countries is a subsidized public education system in which admittance to the upper levels is on the basis of tests that are more easily passed by the children of relatively highly-educated parents; others include a system of government-subsidized access to credit and new technology which is in practice available only to those firms or individuals, urban or rural, industrial or agricultural, which are already relatively wealthy and powerful, and not to the small landowner or tenant farmer or the proprietor of a small business in the informal sector; subsidized public housing, modern medical care, sanitation facilities, etc., that are in practice available only to the relatively wealthy urban dwellers; price controls which keep the price of food below market levels, thus subsidizing the urbanites (rich and poor) at the expense of the rural poor; tax systems which are regressive without that being obvious; and high tariffs on consumer necessities which benefit the few who have control of, or jobs in, the small modern sector of the economy at the expense of the poor who must buy their high-priced goods.[53]

4. Dual Economics. A dual economy situation, often inherited from colonial days and reinforced by development aid policies and actions of TNEs, is often supported by the elite in low-income countries. The political power is often in the hands of those associated with a small modern sector, and policies for its advancement are adopted at the expense of development of the larger traditional sector by means of rural development and aid to the urban poor. Those in the modern sector often base their aspirations and lifestyles on conditions in the high-income countries, which contributes to an ever-growing desire for more for themselves and to resultant disparities in opportunity within their countries.

High levels of military expenditures (often encouraged by arms producers or the government in the United States and other high-income nations) also use up scarce domestic resources and foreign exchange desperately needed for provision of services to the poor.[54] During the decade 1967-1976 the United States was the origin of over half of the value of all arms transfers to low-income nations.[55] The U.S. greatly increased its arms sales to low-income countries from 1971 to 1975.[56]

Lack of emphasis on rural development contributes to the high rates of population growth experienced by many lower-income countries, and the high rates of population growth make it more difficult to raise GNP per capita. Coordinated programs of nutrition, health care, education and general development directed toward the poor, together with voluntary family planning services, could help to reduce the rate of population growth in areas where high rates of growth are contributing to the problems of development.[57]

CONCLUSION

It is clear that the existing socio-economic-political order, within high-income countries, between high- and low-income countries, and within low-income countries, contributes to the wide disparities in lifestyles found intra- and internationally today. Christians, who should be spreading the good news of liberation from sin in Christ to both rich and poor, and working for the establishment of justice, should be aware of those conditions, and should be working to change them, as well as making any necessary changes in their personal lifestyles.

Notes

[1]Ronald J. Sider, *Rich Christians in an Age of Hunger* (Downers Grove, Ill.: InterVarsity Press, 1977), chap. 4.

[2]Although there are problems of improper lifestyles (including institutional problems) in other high-income countries (both capitalist and socialist) as well, I will not discuss them in this paper because they are not the problems we Christians in the United States face and are responsible for. The situation in many other high-income mixed-capitalistic countries is similar to that in the United States, however.

[3]Edward C. Budd, *Inequality and Poverty* (New York: W. W. Norton & Co., 1967), p. xxii. A study for 1969 using different data and methodology found the wealthiest one percent of persons holding 25 percent of net worth and 51 percent of corporate stock (Smith and Franklin, 1974). The ownership of corporate stock is probably not as concentrated now as it was in 1962 or 1969 due to the rise of ownership of stock by pension funds and mutual funds but the *control* over the stock remains highly concentrated.

[4]When the overall unemployment rate rises, the unemployment rates for blacks, women, blue-collar workers, those with low education, and other groups with relatively high unemployment rates tend to rise the most; the average duration of unemployment also rises significantly then, and both of those facts compound the human costs of unem-

ployment. The census bureau estimated that the number of poor families headed by a person unemployed for fifteen weeks or more increased by 223,000 in the recession year of 1975 (U.S. Bureau of the Census, 1977, p. 4). In addition to the loss of income, high unemployment causes many to be unable to fulfill the God-given mandate to work in order to provide for themselves and others. Both of those facts may be related to the increases in illness and suicide observed during periods of high unemployment.

[5]Richard C. Edwards et al., *The Capitalist System* (Englewood Cliffs, N.J.: Prentice-Hall, 1972), pp. 224-226.

[6]Ibid.

[7]Richard A. Musgrave and Peggy B. Musgrave, *Public Finance in Theory and Practice*, 2nd ed. (New York: McGraw-Hill Book Co., 1976), pp. 389-395; Joseph A. Pechman and Benjamin A. Okner, *Who Bears the Tax Burden?* (Washington, D.C.: The Brookings Institution, 1974).

[8]Responsibilities for stewardship and provision for one's own needs are taught in the parable of the talents, Mt. 25:14-30, and in Eph. 4:28, among other places in the Bible. The Mosaic economic laws, if followed, would have provided such opportunities on a regular basis. See George N. Monsma, Jr., "Economic Inequities in the United States," Papers for a Conference on the Inequitable Distribution of Wealth and Power (Classis Lake Erie, Christian Reformed Church, 1977), pp. 2-5; and Sider, pp. 88-93.

[9]Yet another factor in the concentration of wealth exacerbates the problems; that is the concentration of wealth and its attendant economic and political power in the hands of giant corporations. It has been estimated that in 1969 the largest 100 industrial corporations in the United States had 40 percent of the sales and 58 percent of the after-tax profits of all industrial corporations (Edwards, p. 154). The concentration is also very high in other areas, such as banking, finance and insurance, and the concentration within specific industries (e.g., motor vehicles, iron and steel, chemicals, rubber) is much greater. The large size of such corporations gives them significant economic power in relation to, and thus influence on, suppliers, customers, employees, financial institutions, and federal, state, and local governments. For example, they gain influence over consumers through massive advertising and by the limitation on alternative sources of goods inherent in concentrated industries; they gain influence over smaller suppliers by being a major source of sales that is not easily replaced by the supplier if it does not agree to the large firm's terms,

and they gain influence over governments by heavy lobbying, legal and illegal contributions, and the power to influence economic conditions in a particular state or locality, or even the nation as a whole. Even though they are not necessarily technically more efficient than smaller firms, that power enables large corporations to make higher rates of profit, on an average, than small corporations (ibid) and limits the relative opportunity of small firms, whether they be suppliers, customers or competitors of them. That, together with the above-mentioned severe concentration of stockholdings, puts enormous economic and political power into the hands of a relatively small number of stockholders and high-level employees of those corporations, and conversely it limits the power of others. The large size of many modern corporations makes it all the more difficult for most of their employees (even many white-collar employees) to have significant influence on the policies of the corporation and thus to exercise significant stewardship of their own labor (such lack of influence applies to small stockholders as well).

[10]J. K. Galbraith, *The Affluent Society* (Boston: Houghton Mifflin, 1958), especially chaps. 10 and 11; Lee Rainwater, *What Money Buys* (New York: Basic Books, 1974); Richard A. Easterlin, "Does Economic Growth Improve the Human Lot? Some Empirical Evidence," in *Nations and Households in Economic Growth: Essays in Honor of Moses Abramovitz*, ed. Paul A. David and Melvin W. Reder (Palo Alto, Calif.: Stanford University Press, 1974).

[11]Fred Hirsch, *Social Limits to Growth* (Cambridge, Mass.: Harvard Univ. Press, 1976).

[12]This example was developed independently by Lester W. Thurow, in *Generating Inequality* (New York: Basic Books, 1975), pp. 51-128.

[13]Quoted by J. de V. Graaff, in *Theoretical Welfare Economics* (Cambridge: Cambridge Univ. Press, 1957), p. 44.

[14]Galbraith, chap. 11.

[15]Lynde McCormick, "Credit Card Spree Keys a 'Buy Now, Pay Later' World," *Grand Rapids Press*, 18 March 1979, p. 7-D. The article states that one New York bank evades the federal prohibition of sending unsolicited credit cards by calling people and asking, "Would you mind having a VISA card?" and mailing them one if they answer "No."

[16]John W. Sewell et al., *The United States and World Development, Agenda 1977* (New York: Praeger Pub., 1977), pp. 157-158.

[17]Ibid., pp. 147-179.

[18]Robert L. Heilbroner, *An Inquiry into the Human Prospect* (New York: W. W. Norton & Co., 1974), especially chaps. 3 and 4.

[19]Jan Tinbergen, *RIO, Reshaping the International Order* (New York: New American Library, 1976), pp. 97-101.

[20]Ibid., pp. 245-260.

[21]Sewell, pp. 98-101.

[22]Wassily Leontief et al., *The Future of the World Economy* (New York: Oxford Univ. Press, 1977), pp. 64-69.

[23]Sewell, p. 203.

[24]Pierre Uri, *Development without Dependence* (New York: Praeger Pub., 1976), pp. 96-103.

[25]Leontief, p. 65.

[26]David L. McNicol, *Commodity Agreements and Price Stabilization* (Lexington, Mass.: Lexington Books, 1978), p. 18.

[27]Sewell, pp. 195-197; Uri, pp. 96-119; Uri has a particularly extensive discussion of the causes of fluctuations in prices of various types of primary products.

[28]Sewell, p. 95.

[29]McNicol, pp. 1-13, 67, 103-106.

[30]Uri, pp. 104-117; Sewell, pp. 94-97; McNicol, pp. 67-85.

[31]McNicol, pp. 67-85.

[32]Uri, pp. 107-110. Some food aid should still be given, but its amount should be determined by the needs of the recipient nations, not the size of the surpluses in the donor nations, and the aid should be part of an overall plan of development of food production in lower-income nations; in particular, care must be taken not to disrupt incentives for production in the recipient nations (Sewell, pp. 113-117). It might be desirable to have two food reserves, an internationally controlled emergency reserve to be used for cases of severe hunger or famine, and a price-stabilization reserve that could be at least partly held and controlled by the producing countries.

[33]Uri, pp. 134-138.

[34]Sewell, p. 90.

[35]Calculated from data in Sewell, pp. 100, 204, 231.

[36]Hollis Chenery et al., *Redistribution with Growth* (London: Oxford Univ. Press, 1974), pp. 169-170; Uri, pp. 127-138.

[37]H. F. Lydall, *Trade and Employment* (Geneva, Switz.: International Labour Office, 1975), pp. 15-16.

[38]Leontief, p. 63.

[39]Sewell, pp. 230-245.

[40]International Labour Office, *Employment, Growth, and Basic Needs: A One-World Problem* (New York: Praeger Pub., 1977), p. vi.

[41]World Bank, *The Assault on World Poverty* (Baltimore: Johns Hopkins

Univ. Press, 1975), pp. 3-6.

[42]ILO, pp. vi-vii.

[43]Sewell, pp. 21-85.

[44]Calculated from data in Sewell, p. 240, and Roger D. Hansen et al., *The U.S. and World Development, Agenda for Action, 1976* (New York: Praeger Pub., 1976), pp. 186-187.

[45]ILO, p. 129.

[46]Tinbergen, p. 40.

[47]Tinbergen, pp. 193-197, 355-369; Uri, pp. 76-95; ILO, pp. 157-170.

[48]For some information on such differences, see Sewell, especially pp. 156-245, and Chenery, especially pp. 30-37.

[49]Chenery, pp. 6-11.

[50]William Loehr, and John P. Powelson, eds., *Economic Development, Poverty, and Income Distribution* (Boulder, Colo.: Westview Press, 1977), p. 9.

[51]World Bank, pp. 193-261.

[52]Charles Elliott, *Patterns of Poverty in the Third World* (New York: Praeger Pub., 1975), pp. 10-14.

[53]Ibid., pp. 228-262, 313-380.

[54]Sewell, pp. 134-137, 214-217.

[55]U.S. Arms Control and Disarmament Agency, *World Military Expenditures and Arms Transfers,* 1967-1976, publication no. 98 (Washington, D.C.: U.S. Government Printing Office, 1978), p. 157.

[56]Hansen, pp. 186-187.

[57]Bruce F. Johnston, "Food, Health, and Population in Development," *Journal of Economic Literature*, XV, No. 3 (Sept. 1977), 895-899; Lester R. Brown, *In the Human Interest* (New York: W. W. Norton & Co., 1974), pp. 112-127.

CONTRIBUTORS

Elaine M. Amerson lives with her husband, Phil, and two children in Evansville, Ind. She is director of the internship program at Patchwork Central, a county school-board member and professor of communications at Indiana State University at Evansville. Elaine has her doctorate in curriculum and instruction and has lived and taught for twelve years in both Latin America and the U.S.

Howard Claasen is professor of physics at Wheaton College. He chaired the committee that planned the "Human Needs and Global Resources" program at the college and continues to serve on the advisory committee.

Howard Dahl is president of Concord, Inc., a custom metal fabricating business in Fargo, N. Dak., and teaches part-time in the English Department at Concordia College. After graduating from Trinity Evangelical Divinity School. Howard worked for four years with Campus Crusade for Christ. He and his wife, Ann, have one son.

Peter H. Davids, an ordained minister in the Protestant Episcopal Church, was educated at Wheaton College, Trinity Evangelical Divinity School and the University of Manchester. After teaching for two years at Missionshaus Bibelschule Wiedenest in Germany, he returned to the U.S. as a member of the founding faculty of Trinity Episcopal School for Ministry in Ambridge, Pa., where he serves as assistant professor of biblical studies.

Colleen Townsend Evans is wife of Louis Evans, Jr., pastor of National Presbyterian Church and mother of four grown children. She serves on the Hunger Task Force, the Urban Task Force and the core group for the Wrestlers, a class studying world issues from a biblical perspective. Colleen also sits on the Boards of Wooster College, Union Seminary (Richmond) and the Christian College Consortium.

Douglas and Margaret Feaver met in the Inter-Varsity chapter at the University of Toronto. Margaret is a nurse by profession and a homemaker by vocation. Doug is professor of classics at Lehigh University. With their family, they have attended First Presbyterian Church of Bethlehem and have been involved in charismatic home fellowship groups. Because of Doug's work in archaeology, the family has had the opportunity to travel extensively in southern Europe, the Near East and Africa.

Frank E. Gaebelein is headmaster emeritus of the Stony Brook School and former coeditor of *Christianity Today*. He now serves as general editor of the Expositor's Bible Commentary (a twelve-volume series).

Art and Peggy Gish have been trying to live simply for most of their lives. They have three children. Art is the author of *The New Left and Christian Radicalism* (Eerdmans, 1970). *Beyond the Rat Race* (Herald Press, 1973) and *Living in Christian Community* (Herald Press, 1979).

Michael E. Haynes has pursued a dual career in social work and church work. This has led him to his current position as a member of the Commonwealth of Massachusetts Parole Board, and as senior minister of the Twelfth Baptist Church in Roxbury. Haynes remains deeply involved in the life of the Roxbury community.

Walter and Virginia Hearn live in Berkeley, California, where they do all kinds of writing and editing. A former biochemistry professor, Walt has written articles, reviews, poems and chapters in books, and now edits the *Newsletter* of the American Scientific Affiliation. Ginny is the author of two books *What They Did Right: Reflections on Parents by Their Children* and *Our Struggle to Serve: The Stories of 15 Evangelical Women.*

Gladys Hunt lectures and writes books (eleven to date) on subjects which reveal her interests: small group Bible studies, children's literature, women, living for God, Christian reality, and university students. She has been associated with Inter-Varsity Christian Fellowship for over twenty-eight years.

Ronald Klaus is an elder of Living Word Community and ministers in an area including inner-city and suburban Philadelphia and suburban New Jersey. Before joining the ministering team at Living Word in 1976, Ron worked on the staff of Inter-Varsity Christian Fellowship and as assistant professor of engineering at the University of Pennsylvania. Ron and his family live in West Philadelphia.

Virginia MacLaury, along with her husband, president of the Brookings Institution, and two sons, is primarily interested in world hunger and related issues. She serves on the mission committee of National Presbyterian Church and is a member of the Wrestlers class, a group studying world issues from a biblical perspective.

George N. Monsma, Jr. (Ph.D., Princeton) is professor of economics and chairman of the department of economics and business at Calvin College. He is an elder at Sherman Street Christian Reformed Church of Grand Rapids and a board member of Evangelicals for Social Action.

William E. Pannell is assistant professor of evangelism and director of the Theological Studies for Black Pastors Program at Fuller Theological Seminary. He was formerly associated with Tom Skinner in ministries devoted to evangelism throughout black America.

John L. Petersen has been a member of the LaSalle Street Church for nine years. He is a consultant to religious organizations in fund raising, promotion and meeting planning.

David T. Pullen was admitted to the New York State Bar in 1976 after completing studies at Syracuse University College of Law. He practices law in Fillmore, a town in rural western New York state, where he lives with his wife and young son.

Joe Roos is a member and one of the founders of Sojourners Fellowship. He is one of the Fellowship's administrators and publisher of *Sojourners* magazine. Joe was born in Kansas City, Missouri, has a graduate degree in atmospheric science, and has attended seminary.

Arbutus B. Sider, a member in Jubilee Fellowship of Germantown, lives with her husband Ron and three children in an interracial section of Philadelphia. A former school teacher with a Masters degree in psychology, she serves on the executive of Parents Union, an activist, city-wide organization promoting better public education in Philadelphia.

Ronald J. Sider, a graduate of Yale University, now teaches theology at Eastern Baptist Theological Seminary. His most recent books are *Rich Christians in an Age of Hunger* and *Christ and Violence*. He is the president of Evangelicals for Social Action and convenor of the Unit on Ethics and Society of the World Evangelical Fellowship.

Virgil Vogt grew up in India, the son of missionaries. For the past seventeen years he has been a member of Reba Place Fellowship, a communal church in Evanston, Ill. He currently serves as one of the elders of the community.

Carol Westphal is a homemaker and mother of two children. Active in her local Reformed Church, Carol also works with Bread for the World as a volunteer resource person and serves as a member of Discipleship Workshops: Focus on Justice.

Dennis H. Wood, an agricultural economist and lawyer, has worked at Arthur D. Little, Inc. (Boston), as well as in the White House and in the Deputy Secretary's Office of the U.S. State Department. He is now president of Devres, a consulting firm that works on agricultural and rural development projects in developing countries, and its nonprofit affiliate, Development Resources.

DATE DUE